THE ESSENTIALS
OF MYSTICISM

and Other Essays

THE ESSENTIALS
OF MYSTICISM
and Other Essays

Evelyn Underhill

ONEWORLD

OXFORD

THE ESSENTIALS OF MYSTICISM AND OTHER ESSAYS

Oneworld Publications
(Sales and Editorial)
185 Banbury Road
Oxford OX2 7AR
England
http://www.oneworld-publications.com

Oneworld Publications
(US Marketing Office)
160 N. Washington St.
4th Floor, Boston
MA 02114
USA

First published by Oneworld Publications 1995
This edition © Oneworld Publications 1999

Essays previously published in *The Essentials of Mysticism, Mixed Pastures,*
and *The House of the Soul*

ISBN 1–85168–195–7

Cover design by Design Deluxe
Printed in England by Clays Ltd, St Ives plc

CONTENTS

THE ESSENTIALS OF MYSTICISM

WHAT ARE THE TRUE ESSENTIALS OF MYSTICISM? WHEN we have stripped off those features which some mystics accept and some reject – all that is merely due to tradition, temperament or unconscious allegorism – what do we find as the necessary and abiding character of all true mystical experience? This question is really worth asking. For some time much attention has been given to the historical side of mysticism, and some – much less – to its practice. But there has been no clear understanding of the difference between its substance and its accidents: between traditional forms and methods, and the eternal experience which they have mediated. In mystical literature words are frequently confused with things, and symbols with realities; so that much of this literature seems to the reader to refer to some self-consistent and exclusive dream-world, and not to the achievement of universal truth. Thus the strong need for re-statement which is being felt by institutional religion, the necessity of re-translating its truths into symbolism which people can understand and accept today, applies with at least equal force to mysticism. It has become important to disentangle the facts from the ancient formulae used to express them. These formulae have value, because they are genuine attempts to express truth; but they are not themselves that truth, and failure to recognize this distinction has caused a good deal of misunderstanding. Thus, on its philosophic and theological side, the mysticism of Western Europe is tightly entwined with the patristic and medieval presentation of Christianity; and this presentation, though full of noble poetry, is now difficult if not impossible to adjust to our conceptions of the universe. Again, on its personal side mysticism is a department of psychology. Now psychology is changing under our eyes; already we see our mental life in a new perspective and tend to describe it under new forms. Our ways of describing and interpreting spiritual experience must change with the rest, if we are to keep in touch with reality; though the experience itself is unchanged.

So we are forced to ask ourselves, what is the essential element in spiritual experience? Which of the many states and revelations described by the mystics are integral parts of it; and what do these states and degrees come to, when we describe them in the current phraseology and strip off the monastic robes in which they are usually dressed? What elements are due to the suggestions of tradition, to conscious or unconscious symbolism, to the misinterpretation of emotion, to the invasion of cravings from the lower centres, or the disguised fulfilment of an unconscious wish? And when all these channels of illusion have been blocked, what is left? This will be a difficult and often painful enquiry. But it is an enquiry which ought to be faced by all who believe in the validity of human spiritual experience, in order that their faith may be established on a firm basis and disentangled from those unreal and impermanent elements which are certainly destined to destruction, and with which it is at present too often confused. I am sure that at the present moment we serve the highest interests of the soul best by subjecting the whole mass of material which is called 'mysticism' to an inexorable criticism. Only by inflicting the faithful wounds of a friend can we save the science of the inner life from mutilation at the hands of the psychologists.

We will begin, then, with the central fact of the mystic's experience. This central fact, it seems to me, is an overwhelming consciousness of God and of one's own soul: a consciousness which absorbs or eclipses all other centres of interest. It is said that St Francis of Assisi, praying in the house of Bernard of Quintavalle, was heard to say again and again: 'My God! my God! What art Thou? And what am I?' Though the words come from St Augustine, they well represent his mental attitude. This was the only question which he thought worth asking; and it is the question which all mystics ask at the beginning and sometimes answer at the end of their quest. Hence we must put first among our essentials the clear conviction of a living God as the primary interest of consciousness, and of a personal self capable of communion with Him. Having said this, however, we may allow that the widest latitude is possible in mystics' conception of their Deity. At best this conception will be symbolic; their experience, if genuine, will far transcend the symbols they employ. 'God', says the author of *The Cloud of Unknowing*, 'may well be loved but not thought.' Credal forms, therefore, can only be for mystics a scaffold by which they ascend. We are even bound, I think, to confess that the overt recognition of that which orthodox Christians generally mean by a personal God is not essential. On the contrary, where it takes a crudely anthropomorphic form, the idea of personality may be a disadvantage, opening the way for the intrusion of disguised emotions and desires. In the highest experiences of the greatest mystics the personal category appears to be transcended. 'The light in the soul which is increate', says Eckhart, 'is not satisfied with the three Persons, in so far as each subsists in its difference . . . but it is determined to know whence this Being comes, to penetrate into the Simple Ground, into the Silent Desert within which never any difference has lain.'

The all-inclusive One is beyond all partial apprehensions, though the true values which those apprehensions represent are conserved in it. However pantheistic mystics may be on the one hand, however absolutist on the other, their communion with God is always personal in this sense: it is communion with a living Reality, an object of love, capable of response, which demands and receives from them a total self-donation. This sense of a double movement, a self-giving on the divine side answering to the self-giving on the human side, is found in all great mysticism. It has, of course, lent itself to emotional exaggeration, but in its pure form seems an integral part of human apprehension of Reality. Even where it conflicts with the mystic's philosophy – as in Hinduism and Neoplatonism – it is still present. It is curious to note, for instance, how

Plotinus, after safeguarding his Absolute One from every qualification, excluding it from all categories, defining it only by the icy method of negation, suddenly breaks away into the language of ardent feeling when he comes to describe that ecstasy in which he touched the truth. Then he speaks of 'the veritable love, the sharp desire' which possessed him, appealing to the experience of those fellow mystics who have 'caught fire, and found the splendour there.' These, he says, have 'felt burning within themselves the flame of love for what is there to know – the passion of the lover resting on the bosom of his love.'

So we may say that the particular mental image which mystics form of their objective, the traditional theology they accept, is not essential. Since it is never adequate, the degree of its inadequacy is of secondary importance. Though some creeds have proved more helpful to mystics than others, they are found fully developed in every great religion. We cannot honestly say that there is any wide difference between the Brahman, Súfí or Christian mystic at their best. They are far more like each other than they are like the average believer in their several creeds. What is essential is the way mystics feel about their Deity, and about their own relation with it; for this adoring and all-possessing consciousness of the rich and complete divine life over against the self's life, and of the possible achievement of a level of being, a sublimation of the self, wherein we are perfectly united with it, may fairly be written down as a necessary element of all mystical life. This is the common factor that unites those apparently incompatible views of the universe which have been claimed at one time or another as mystical. Their mystical quality abides wholly in the temper of the self who adopts them. Mystics may be transcendentalists: but if so, it is because their intuition of the divine is so lofty that it cannot be expressed by means of any intellectual concept, and they are bound to say with Ruysbroeck, 'He is neither This nor That.' They may be unanimists; but if they are, it is because they find in other people – more, in the whole web of life – that mysterious living essence which is a mode of God's existence, and which they love, seek and recognize everywhere. 'How shall I find words for the beauty of my Beloved? For He is merged in all beauty,' says Kabir. 'His colour is in all the pictures of the world, and it bewitches the body and the mind.' They may be – often are – sacramentalists; but if so, only because the symbol or the sacrament helps them to touch God. So St Thomas:

> Adoro te devote, latens Deitas,
> Quæ sub his figuris vere latitas.

The moment mystics suspect that any of these things are obstacles instead of means, they reject them, to the scandal of those who habitually confuse the image with the reality.

Thus we get the temperamental symbolist, quietist, nature-mystic, or transcendentalist. We get Plotinus rapt to the 'bare pure One'; St Augustine's impassioned communion with Perfect Beauty; Eckhart declaring his achievement of the 'wilderness of God'; Jacopone da Todi prostrate in adoration before the 'Love that gives all things form'; Ruysbroeck describing his achievement of 'that wayless abyss of fathomless beatitude where the Trinity of divine persons possess their nature in the essential Unity;' Jacob Boehme gazing into the fire-world and there finding the living heart of the universe; Kabir listening to the rhythmic music of Reality, and seeing the worlds told like beads within the Being of God. And at the opposite pole we find Mechthild of Magdeburg's amorous conversations with her 'heavenly Bridegroom'; the many mystical experiences connected with the Eucharist; the Súfí's enraptured description of God as the 'Matchless Chalice and the Sovereign Wine'; and the narrow intensity and emotional raptures of contemplatives of the type of Richard Rolle. We cannot refuse the title of mystic to any of these, because in every case their aim is union between God and the soul. This is the one essential of mysticism, and there are as many ways from one term to the other as there are variations in the human spirit. But, on the other hand, when anybody speaking of mysticism proposes an object that is less than God – increase of knowledge, of health, of happiness, occultism, intercourse with spirits, supernormal experience in general – then we may begin to suspect that we are off the track,

Now we come to the next group of essentials: the necessary acts and dispositions of the mystics themselves, the development which takes place in them – the psychological facts, that is to say, which are represented by the so-called 'mystic way'. The mystic way is best understood as a process of sublimation, which carries the correspondences of the self with the universe up to higher levels than those on which our normal consciousness works. Just as the normal consciousness stands over against the unconscious, which, with its buried impulses and its primitive and infantile cravings, represents a cruder reaction of the organism to the external world; so does the developed mystical life stand over against normal consciousness, with its preoccupations and its web of illusions encouraging the animal will-to-dominate and the animal will-to-live. Normal consciousness sorts out some elements from the mass of experiences beating at our doors and constructs from them a certain order; but this order lacks any deep meaning or true cohesion, because normal consciousness is incapable of apprehending the underlying reality from which these scattered experiences proceed. The claim of the mystical consciousness is to a closer reading of truth, to an apprehension of the divine unifying principle behind appearance. 'The One', says Plotinus, 'is present everywhere and absent only from those unable to perceive it'; and when we *do* perceive it we 'have another life . . . attaining the aim of our existence, and our rest'. To know this at first hand – not to guess, believe or accept, but to be certain – is the highest achievement of human consciousness, and the ultimate object of mysticism. How is it done?

There are two ways of attacking this problem which may conceivably help us. The first consists in a comparison of the declarations of different mystics, and a sorting out of those elements which they have in common: a careful watch being kept, of course, for the results of conscious or unconscious imitation, tradition and theological preconceptions. In this way we get some firsthand evidence of factors which are at any rate usually present, and may possibly be essential. The second line of enquiry consists in a re-translation into psychological terms of these mystical declarations, when many will reveal the relation in which they stand to the psychic life of human beings.

Reviewing the firsthand declarations of the mystics, we inevitably notice one prominent feature: the frequency with which they break up their experience into three phases. Sometimes they regard these objectively, and speak of three worlds or three aspects of God of which they become successively aware. Sometimes they regard them subjectively, and speak of three stages of growth through which they pass, such as those of Beginner, Proficient and Perfect; or of phases of spiritual progress in which we first meditate upon Reality, then contemplate Reality, and at last are united with Reality. But among the most widely separated mystics of the East and West, this threefold experience can nearly always be traced. There are, of course, obvious dangers in attaching absolute value to number-schemes of this kind. Numbers have an uncanny power over the human mind; once let a symbolic character be attributed to them, and the temptation to make them fit the facts at all costs becomes overwhelming. We all know that the number 'three' has a long religious history, and are therefore inclined to look with suspicion on its claim to interpret the mystic life. At the same time there are other significant numbers – such as 'seven' and 'ten' – which have never gained equal currency as the bases of mystical formulae. We may agree that the medieval mystics found the threefold division of spiritual experience in Neoplatonism; but we must also agree that a formula of this kind is not likely to survive for nearly 2000 years unless it agrees with the facts. Those who use it with the greatest conviction are not theorists. They are the practical mystics, who are intent on making maps of the regions into which they have penetrated.

Moreover, this is no mere question of handing on one single tradition. The mystics describe their movement from appearance to reality in many different ways, and use many incompatible religious symbols. The one constant factor is the discrimination of three phases of consciousness, no more, no less, in which we can recognize certain common characteristics. 'There are', says Philo, 'three kinds of life: life as it concerns God, life as it concerns the creature, and a third intermediate life, a mixture of the former two.' Consistently with this, Plotinus speaks of three descending phases or principles of Divine Reality: the Godhead, or absolute and unconditioned One; its manifestation as *Nous*, the Divine Mind or Spirit which inspires the 'intelligible' and eternal world; and *Psyche*, the life or soul of the physical universe. Human beings, normally in correspondence with this physical world of succession and change, may by spiritual intuition achieve the first consciousness of the eternal world of spiritual values, in which indeed the apex of the human soul already dwells; and in brief moments of ecstatic vision may rise above this to communion with its source, the Absolute One.

There you have the mystic's vision of the universe, and the mystic's way of purification, enlightenment and ecstasy, bringing new and deeper knowledge of reality as the self's interest, urged by its loving desire of the

Ultimate, is shifted from sense to soul, from soul to spirit. There is here no harsh dualism, no turning from a bad material world to a good spiritual world. We are invited to one gradual undivided process of sublimation, penetrating ever more deeply into the reality of the universe, to find at last 'that One who is present everywhere and absent only from those who do not perceive Him'. What we behold, that we are: citizens, according to our own will and desire, of the surface world of the senses, the deeper world of life, or the ultimate world of spiritual reality.

An almost identical doctrine appears in the Upanishads. At the heart of reality is Brahma, 'other than the known, and above the unknown.' His manifestation is Ananda, that spiritual world which is the true object of aesthetic passion and religious contemplation. From it life and consciousness are born, in it they have their being, to it they must return. Finally, there is the world-process as we know it, which represents Ananda taking form. So too the mystic Kabir, who represents an opposition to the Vedantic philosophy, says: 'From beyond the Infinite the Infinite comes, and from the Infinite the finite extends.' And again: 'Some contemplate the formless and others meditate on form but the wise man knows that Brahma is beyond both.' Here we have the finite world of becoming, the infinite world of being, and Brahma, the Unconditioned Absolute, exceeding and including all. Yet, as Kabir distinctly declares again and again, there are no fences between these aspects of the universe. When we come to the root of reality we find that 'Conditioned and unconditioned are but one word', the difference is in our own degree of awareness.

Compare with this three of the great medieval Catholic mystics: that acute psychologist Richard of St Victor, the ardent poet and contemplative Jacopone da Todi, and the profound Ruysbroeck. Richard of St Victor says that there are three phases in the contemplative consciousness. The first is called dilation of mind, enlarging and deepening our vision of the world. The next is elevation of mind, in which we behold the realities which are above ourselves. The third is ecstasy, in which the mind is carried up to contact with truth in its pure simplicity. This is really the universe of Plotinus translated into subjective terms. So, too, Jacopone da Todi says in the symbolism of his day that three heavens are open to human beings. They must climb from one to the other; it is hard work, but love and longing press them on. First when the mind has achieved self-conquest, the 'starry heaven' of multiplicity is revealed to it. Its darkness is lit by scattered lights; points of reality pierce the sky. Next, it achieves the 'crystalline heaven' of lucid contemplation, where the soul is conformed to the rhythm of the divine life, and by its loving intuition apprehends God under veils. Lastly, in ecstasy it may be lifted to that ineffable state which he calls the 'hidden heaven', where it enjoys a vision of imageless reality and 'enters into possession of all that is God'. Ruysbroeck says that he has experienced three orders of reality: the natural world, theatre of our moral struggle; the essential world, where God and eternity are indeed known, but by intermediaries; and the super-essential world, where without intermediary, and beyond all separation, 'above reason and without reason', the soul is united to 'the glorious and absolute One'.

Take, again, a totally different mystic, Jacob Boehme. He says that he saw in the Divine Essence three principles or aspects. The first he calls 'the deepest Deity, without and beyond Nature', and the next its manifestation in the eternal light-world. The third is that outer world in which we dwell according to the body, which is a manifestation, image or similitude of the Eternal. 'And we are thus', he says, 'to understand reality as a threefold being, or three worlds *in one another.*' We observe again the absence of watertight compartments. The whole of reality is present in every part of it; and the power of correspondence with all these aspects of it is latent in human beings. 'If one sees a right man', says Boehme again, 'he may say, I see here three worlds standing.'

We have now to distinguish the essential element in all this. How does it correspond with psychological facts? Some mystics, like Richard of St Victor, have frankly exhibited its subjective side and so helped us to translate the statements of their fellows. Thus Dionysius the Areopagite says in a celebrated passage: 'Threefold is the way to God. The first is the way of purification, in which the mind is inclined to learn true wisdom. The second is the way of illumination, in which the mind by contemplation is kindled to the burning of love. The third is the way of union, in which the mind by understanding, reason and spirit is led up by God alone.' This formula restates the Plotinian law; for the 'contemplation' of Dionysius is the 'spiritual intuition' of Plotinus, which inducts human beings into the intelligible world; his 'union' is the Plotinian ecstatic vision of the One. It profoundly impressed the later Christian mystics, and has long been accepted as the classic description of spiritual growth, because it has been found again and again to answer to experience. It is therefore worth our while to examine it with some care.

We notice first how gentle, gradual and natural is the process of sublimation that Dionysius demands of us. According to him, the mystic life is a life centred on reality: the life that first seeks reality without flinching, then loves and adores the reality perceived, and at last, wholly surrendered to it, is 'led by God alone'. First the self is 'inclined to learn true wisdom.' It awakes to new needs, is cured of its belief in sham values, and distinguishes between real and unreal objects of desire. That craving for more life and more love which lies at the very heart of our selfhood, here slips from the charmed circle of the senses into a wider air. When this happens abruptly it is called 'conversion' and may then have the character of a psychic convulsion and be accompanied by various secondary psychological phenomena. But often it comes without observation. Here the essentials are a desire and a disillusionment sufficiently strong to overcome our natural sloth, our primitive horror of change. 'The first beginning of all things is a craving', says Boehme; 'we are creatures of will and desire.' The divine discontent, the hunger for reality and the unwillingness to be satisfied with the purely animal or the purely social level of consciousness, is the first essential stage in the development of the mystical consciousness.

So the self is either suddenly or gradually inclined

to 'true wisdom'; and this change of angle affects the whole character, not only or indeed specially the intellectual outlook but the ethical outlook too. This is the meaning of 'purgation'. False ways of feeling and thinking, established complexes which have acquired for us an almost sacred character and governed, though we knew it not, all our reactions to life – these must be broken up. That mental and moral sloth which keeps us so comfortably wrapped in unrealities must go. This phase in the mystic's growth has been specially emphasized and worked out by the Christian mystics, who have made considerable additions to the philosophy and natural history of the soul. The Christian sense of sin and conception of charity, the Christian notion of humility as a finding of our true level, an exchanging of the unreal standards of egoism for the disconcerting realities of life seen from the angle of eternity; the steadfast refusal to tolerate any claim to spirituality which is not solidly based on moral values, or which is divorced from the spirit of tenderness and love – all this has immensely enriched the mysticism of the West, and filled up some of the gaps left by Neoplatonism.

It is characteristic of Christianity that, addressing itself to all people – not, as Neoplatonism tended to do, to the superior person – and offering to all people participation in eternal life, it takes human nature as it is and works from the bottom up, instead of beginning at a level which only a few of the race attain. Christianity perceived how deeply normal people are enslaved by the unconscious, how great a moral struggle is needed for their emancipation. Hence it concentrated on the first stage of purgation, and gave it new meaning and depth. The monastic rule of poverty, chastity and obedience – and we must remember that the original aim of monasticism was to provide a setting in which the mystical life could be lived – aims at the removal of those self-centred desires and attachments which chain consciousness to a personal instead of a universal life. Those who no longer crave for personal possessions, pleasures or powers, are very near to perfect liberty. Their attention is freed from its usual concentration on the self's immediate interests, and at once they see the universe in a new, more valid, because disinterested light.

> Povertate è nulla avere
> e nulla cosa poi volere
> ed omne cosa possedere
> en spirito de libertade.

Yet this positive moral purity which Christians declared necessary to the spiritual life was not centred on a lofty aloofness from human failings, but on a self-giving and disinterested love, the complete abolition of egoism. This alone, it declared, could get rid of that inward disharmony – one aspect of the universal conflict between the instinctive and the rational life – which Boehme called the 'powerful contrarium' warring with the soul.

Now this 'perfect charity in life surrendered', however attained, is an essential character of the true mystic; without it, contemplation is an impossibility or a sham. But when we come to the means by which it is to be attained, we re-enter the region of controversy; for here we are at once confronted by the problem of asceticism, and its connection with mysticism – perhaps the largest and most difficult of the questions now facing those who are concerned with the re-statement of the laws of the spiritual life. Originally regarded as a gymnastic of the soul, an education in those 'manly' virtues of self-denial and endurance without which the spiritual life is merely an exquisite form of hedonism, asceticism was identified by Christian thought with the idea of mortification; the killing out of all those impulses which deflect the soul from the straight path to God.

For the true mystic, it is never more than a means to an end, and is often thrown aside when that end is attained. Its necessity is therefore a purely practical question. Fasting and watching may help one to dominate unruly instincts, and so attain a sharper and purer concentration on God; but make another so hungry and sleepy that he or she can think of nothing else. Thus Jacopone da Todi said of his own early austerities that they resulted chiefly in indigestion, insomnia and colds in the head; whilst John Wesley found in fasting a positive spiritual good. Some ascetic practices again are almost certainly disguised indulgences of those very cravings which they are supposed to kill, but in fact merely repress. Others – such as hair shirts, chains, and so forth – depended for their meaning on a medieval view of the body and of the virtues of physical pain which is practically extinct, and now seems to most of us utterly artificial. No one will deny that austerity is better than luxury for the spiritual life; but perfect detachment of the will and senses can be achieved without resort to merely physical expedients by those living normally in the world, and this is the essential thing.

The true asceticism is a gymnastic not of the body, but of the mind. It involves training in the art of recollection; the concentration of thought, will, and love upon the eternal realities which we commonly ignore. Embryo contemplatives, if their spiritual vision is indeed to be enlarged, and their minds kindled, as Dionysius says, to 'the burning of love', must acquire and keep a special state of inward poise, an attitude of attention, which is best described as 'the state of prayer'; that same condition which George Fox called 'keeping in the Universal Spirit'. If we do not attend to reality, we are not likely to perceive it. The readjustments which will make this attention natural and habitual are a phase in the inward conflict for the redemption of consciousness from its lower and partial attachments. This conflict is no dream. It means hard work: mental and moral discipline of the sternest kind. The downward drag is incessant, and can be combated only by those who are clearly aware of it, and are willing to sacrifice lower interests and joys to the demands of the spiritual life. In this sense mortification is an integral part of the 'purgative way'. Unless the self's 'inclination to true wisdom' is strong enough to inspire these costing and heroic efforts, its spiritual cravings do not deserve the name of mysticism.

These, then, seem essential factors in the readjustment which the mystics call purgation. We go on to their next stage, the so-called 'way of illumination'. Here, says Dionysius, the mind is kindled by contemplation to the burning of love. There is a mental and an emotional enhancement, whereby the self apprehends the reality it has sought, whether under the veils of religion, philosophy, or nature-mysticism. Many mystics have made clear statements about this phase in human transcendence. Thus the Upanishads invite us to 'know everything in the universe as enveloped in God'. 'When the purified seeker', says Plato, 'comes to the end, he will suddenly perceive a nature of wondrous beauty . . . Beauty absolute, separate, simple and ever-lasting.' His follower Plotinus says that by spiritual intuition human beings, 'wrought into harmony with the Supreme', enter into communion with *Nous*, the 'intelligible world' of eternal realities – that splendour yonder which is their home; and further that this light, shining upon the soul, enlightens it, makes it a member of the spiritual order, and so 'transforms the furnace of this world into a garden of flowers'. Ruysbroeck declares that this eternal world 'is not God, but it is the light in which we see Him'. Jacopone da Todi says that the self, achieving the crystalline heaven, 'feels itself to be a part of all things', because it has annihilated its separate will and is conformed to the movement of the divine life. Kabir says: 'The middle region of the sky, wherein the Spirit dwelleth, is radiant with the music of light.' Boehme calls it the 'light-world proceeding from the fire-world', and says it is the origin of that outward world in which we dwell. 'This light', he says, 'shines through and through all, but is only apprehended by that which unites itself thereto.'

It seems to me fairly clear that these, and many other descriptions I cannot now quote, refer to an identical state of consciousness, which might be called an experience of eternity, but not of the Eternal One. I say 'an experience', not merely a mental perception. Contemplation, which is the traditional name for that concentrated attention in which this phase of reality is revealed, is an activity of all our powers: the heart, the will, the mind. Dionysius emphasizes the ardent love which this revelation of reality calls forth and which is indeed a condition of our apprehension of it, for the cold gaze of the metaphysician cannot attain it, unless he be a lover and a mystic too. 'By love He may be gotten and holden, by thought never', says the author of *The Cloud of Unknowing*. (It is only through the mood of humble and loving receptivity in which the artist perceives beauty, that the human spirit can apprehend a reality which is greater than itself. The many declarations about noughting, poverty and 'holy nothingness' refer to this. The meek and poor of spirit really are the inheritors of eternity.)

So we may place the attitude of selfless adoration, the single-hearted passion of the soul, among the essentials of the mystic in the illuminated way. A very wide range of mystical experiences must be attributed to this second stage in human spiritual growth. Some at least of its secrets are known to all who are capable of aesthetic passion; who, in the presence of beauty, know themselves to stand upon the fringe of another plane of being, where the elements of common life are given new colour and value, and its apparent disharmonies are resolved. So, too, that deep sense of a divine companionship which many ardent souls achieve in prayer is a true if transitory experience of illumination.

We shall probably be right in assuming that the enormous majority of mystics never get beyond this level of consciousness. Certainly a large number of religious writers on mysticism attribute to its higher and more personal manifestations the names of 'divine union' and 'unitive life', thereby adding to the difficulty of classifying spiritual states and showing themselves unaware of the great distinction which such full-grown mystics as Plotinus, Jacopone da Todi or Ruysbroeck describe as existing between this 'middle heaven' and the ecstatic vision of the One which alone really satisfies their thirst for truth. Thus Jacopone at first uses the strongest unitive language to describe that rapturous and emotional intercourse with Divine Love which characterized his middle period; but when he at last achieves the vision of the Absolute, he confesses that he was in error in supposing that it was indeed the Truth whom he thus saw and worshipped under veils.

> Or, parme, fo fallanza,
> non se' quel che credea,
> tenendo non avea
> vertá senza errore.

Thus Ruysbroeck attributes to the contemplative life 'the inward and upward-going ways by which one may pass into the Presence of God', but distinguishes these from that super-essential life wherein 'we are swallowed up, beyond reason and above reason, in the deep quiet of the Godhead which is never moved'.

All the personal raptures of devotional mysticism, all the nature-mystic's joyous consciousness of God in creation, Blake's 'world of imagination and vision', the 'coloured land' of AE (George Russell), the Súfí's 'tavern on the way' where he is refreshed by a draught of supersensual wine, belong to the way of illumination. For the Christian mystic the world into which it inducts him is, pre-eminently, the sphere of the divine Logos-Christ, fount of creation and source of all beauty, the hidden Steersman who guides and upholds the phenomenal world:

> Splendor che dona a tutto 'l mondo luce,
> amor, Iesú, de li angeli belleza,
> cielo e terra per te si conduce
> e splende in tutte cose tua fattezza.

Here the reality behind appearance is still mediated to mystics under symbols and forms. The variation of these symbols is great; their adoring gaze now finds new life and significance in the appearances of nature, the creations of music and of art, the imagery of religion and philosophy, and reality speaks to them through their own credal conceptions. But absolute value cannot be attributed to any of these, even the most sacred: they change, yet the experience remains. Thus an identical consciousness of close communion with God is obtained by the non-sacramental Quakers in their silence and by the sacramental Catholics in the Eucharist. The Christian contemplatives' sense of personal intercourse with the divine as manifest in the incarnate Christ is hard to distinguish from that of the Hindu Vaishnavites, when we have allowed for the different constituents of their apperceiving mass:

Dark, dark the far Unknown and closed the way
To thought and speech; silent the Scriptures; yea,
No word the Vedas say.
Not thus the Manifest. How fair! how near!
Gone is our thirst if only He appear –
He, to the heart so dear.

So, too, the Súfí mystic who has learned to say: 'I never saw anything without seeing God therein'; Kabir exclaiming: 'I have stilled my restless mind, and my heart is radiant; for in Thatness I have seen beyond Thatness, in company I have seen the Comrade Himself'; the Neoplatonist rapt in contemplation of the intelligible world 'yonder'; Brother Lawrence doing his cooking in the presence of God – all reveal under analysis an identical type of consciousness. This consciousness is the essential; the symbols under which the self apprehends it are not.

Among these symbols we must reckon a large number of the secondary phenomena of mysticism: divine visions and voices, and other dramatizations of the self's apprehensions and desires. The best mystics have always recognized the doubtful nature of these so-called divine revelations and favours, and have tried again and again to set up tests for discerning those which really 'come from God' – i.e. mediate a valid spiritual experience. Personally, I think very few of these phenomena are mystical in the true sense. Just as our normal consciousness is more or less at the mercy of invasions from the unconscious region, of impulses which we fail to trace to their true origin, so too the mystical consciousness is perpetually open to invasion from the lower centres. These invasions are not always understood by the mystic. Obvious examples are the erotic raptures of the Súfí poets, and the emotional, even amorous relations in which many Christian ascetics believe themselves to stand to Christ or Our Lady. The Holy Ghost saying to Angela of Foligno, 'I love you better than any other woman in the vale of Spoleto'; the human raptures of Mechthild of Magdeburg with her Bridegroom; St Bernard's attitude to the Virgin; the passionate love-songs of Jacopone da Todi; the mystical marriage of St Catherine of Siena; St Teresa's 'wound of love' – these, and many similar episodes, demand no supernatural explanation, and add nothing to our knowledge of the work of the Spirit in the human soul.

So, too, the infantile craving for a sheltering and protective love finds expression over and over again in mystical literature, and satisfaction in the states of consciousness which it has induced. The innate longing of the self for more life, more love, an ever greater and fuller experience, attains a complete realization in the lofty mystical state called union with God. But failing this full achievement, the self is capable of offering itself many disguised satisfactions; and among these disguised satisfactions we must reckon at least the majority of 'divine favours' enjoyed by contemplatives of an emotional type. Whatever the essence of mysticism may turn out to be, it is well to recognize these lapses to lower levels as among the least fortunate of its accidents.

We come to the third stage, the true goal of mystic experience; the intuitive contact with that Ultimate Reality which theologians mean by the Godhead and philosophers by the Absolute, a contact in which, as

Richard of St Victor says, 'the soul gazes upon Truth without any veils of creatures – not in a mirror darkly, but in its pure simplicity'. The claim to this is the loftiest claim that can be made by human consciousness. There is little we can say of it because there is little we know, save that the vision or experience is always the vision or experience of a unity which reconciles all opposites, and fulfils all humanity's highest intuitions of reality. 'Be lost altogether in Brahma like an arrow that has completely penetrated its target', say the Upanishads. This self-loss, says Dionysius the Areopagite, is the divine initiation wherein we 'pass beyond the topmost altitudes of the holy ascent, and leave behind all divine illumination and voices and heavenly utterances; and plunge into the darkness where truly dwells, as Scripture saith, that One which is beyond all things'.

Some recent theologians have tried to separate the conceptions of God and of the Absolute, but mystics never do this, though some of the most clear-sighted, such as Meister Eckhart, have separated that unconditioned Godhead known in ecstasy from the personal God who is the object of devotional religion, and who represents a humanization of reality. When the great mystics achieve the 'still, glorious, and absolute Oneness' which finally satisfies their thirst for truth – the 'point where all lines meet and show their meaning' – they generally confess how symbolic was the object of their earlier devotion, how partial their supposed communion with the Divine. Thus Jacopone da Todi – exact and orthodox Catholic though he was – when he reached 'the hidden heaven', discovered and boldly declared the approximate character of all his previous

conceptions of, and communion with God, the great
extent to which subjective elements had entered into his
experience. In the great ode which celebrates his
ecstatic vision of Truth, when 'ineffable love, imageless
goodness, measureless light' at last shone in his heart, he
says: 'I thought I knew Thee, tasted Thee, saw Thee
under image: believing I held Thee in Thy completeness
I was filled with delight and unmeasured love. But *now* I
see I was mistaken – Thou art not as I thought and
firmly held.' So Tauler says that compared with the
warm colour and multiplicity of devotional experience,
the very Godhead is a 'rich nought', a 'bare pure ground';
and Ruysbroeck that it is 'an unwalled world', 'neither
this nor that'. 'This fruition of God', he says again, 'is a
still and glorious and essential Oneness beyond the
differentiation of the Persons, where there is neither an
outpouring nor an indrawing of God, but the Persons
are still and one in fruitful love, in calm and glorious
unity. . . . There is God our fruition and His own, in an
eternal and fathomless bliss.'

'How, then, am I to love the Godhead?' says
Eckhart. 'Thou shalt love Him as He is: not as a God,
not as a Spirit, not as a Person, not as an image, but as a
sheer pure One. And in this One we are to sink from
nothing to nothing, so help us God.' 'This consciousness
of the One', says Plotinus, 'comes not by knowledge, but
by an actual Presence superior to any knowing. To have
it, the soul must rise above knowledge, above all its
wandering from its unity.' He goes on to explain that all
partial objects of love and contemplation, even beauty
and goodness themselves, are lower than this, springing
from the One as light from the sun. To see the disc, we

must put on smoked glasses, shut off the rays, and submit to the 'radiant darkness' which enters so frequently into mystical descriptions of the Absolute.

It is an interesting question whether this consummation of the mystic way need involve that suppression of the surface-consciousness which is called ecstasy. The majority of mystics think that it must; and probably it is almost inevitable that so great a concentration and so lofty an intuition should for the time it lasts drive all other forms of awareness from the field. Even simple contemplation cannot be achieved without some deliberate stilling of the senses, a deliberate focusing of our vagrant attention, which abolishes self-consciousness while it lasts. This is the way that our mental machinery works; but this should not make us regard trance-states as any part of the essence of mysticism. The ecstatic condition is no guarantee of mystic vision. It is frequently pathological, and is often found along with other abnormal conditions in emotional visionaries whose revelations have no ultimate characteristics. It is, however, just as uncritical to assume that ecstasy is necessarily a pathological symptom, as it is to assume that it is necessarily a mystic state. We have a test which we can apply to the ecstatic, which separates the results of nervous disorder from those of spiritual transcendence. 'What fruit dost thou bring back from this thy vision?' is the final question which Jacopone da Todi addresses to the mystic's soul. And the answer is: 'An ordered life in every state.'

True mystics in their ecstasy have seen, however obscurely, the key of the universe: 'la forma universal di questo nodo'. Hence they have a clue by which to live.

Reality has become real to them; and there are no others of whom we can fully say that. So, ordered correspondence with each level of existence, physical and spiritual, successive and eternal – a practical realization of the proportions of life – is the guarantee of the genuine character of that sublimation of consciousness which is called the mystic way; and this distinguishes it from the fantasies of psychic illness or the disguised self-indulgences of the dream-world. Real mystics are not selfish visionaries. They grow in vigour as they draw nearer and nearer the sources of true life, and their goal is only reached when they participate in the creative energies of the divine nature. The perfect human being, says the Súfí, must not only die into God in ecstasy (fana), but abide in and with Him (baqa), manifesting His truth in the world of time. He or she is called to a life more active, because more contemplative, than that of other people: to fulfil the monastic ideal of a balanced career of work and prayer. 'Then only is our life a *whole*', says Ruysbroeck, 'when contemplation and work dwell in us side by side, and we are perfectly in both of them at once.'

Plotinus speaks in the same sense under another image in one of his most celebrated passages: 'We always move round the One, but we do not always fix our gaze upon it. We are like a choir of singers standing round the conductor, who do not always sing in time, because their attention is diverted to some external object. When they look at the conductor, they sing well and are really with him. So we always move round the One. If we did not, we should dissolve and cease to exist. But we do not always look towards the One. When we do, we attain the end of our existence and our rest; and we no longer sing out of tune, but form in truth a divine choir about the One.' In this conception of human privilege and duty we have the indestructible essence of mysticism.

THE MYSTIC AND THE
CORPORATE LIFE

❁

ONE OF THE COMMONEST OF THE CRITICISMS WHICH
are brought against the mystics is that they
represent an unsocial type of religion; that their spiritual
enthusiasms are personal and individual, and that they
do not share or value the corporate life and institutions
of the Church or community to which they belong. Yet,
as a matter of fact, the relation that does and should
exist between personal religion and the corporate life of
the Church frequently appears in them in a peculiarly
intense, a peculiarly interesting form; and in their lives,
perhaps, more easily than elsewhere, we may discern the
principles which do or should govern the relation of the
individual to the community.

In true mystics, who are so often and so wrongly
called 'religious individualists', we see personal religion
raised to its highest power. If we accept their experience
as genuine, it involves an intercourse with the spiritual
world, an awareness of it, which transcends the normal
experience, and appears to be independent of the
general religious consciousness of the community to
which they belong. Mystics speak with God as persons

with a Person, and not as members of a group. They live by an immediate knowledge far more than by belief; by a knowledge achieved in those hours of direct, unmediated intercourse with the Transcendent when, as they say, they were 'in union with God'. The certitude then gained – a certitude which they cannot impart, and which is not generally diffused – governs all their reactions to the universe. It even persists and upholds them in those terrible hours of darkness when all their sense of spiritual reality is taken away.

Such a personality as this seems at first sight to stand in little need of the support which the smaller nature, the more languid religious consciousness, receives from the corporate spirit. By the very term 'mystic' we indicate a certain aloofness from the crowd, suggest that they are in possession of a secret which the community as a whole does not and cannot share, that they live at levels to which others cannot rise. I think that much of the distrust with which they are often regarded comes from this sense of their independence of the herd, their apparent separation from the often clumsy and always symbolic methods of institutional religion, and the further fact that their own methods and results cannot be criticized or checked by those who have not shared them. 'I spake as I saw,' said David; and those who did not see can only preserve a respectful or an exasperated silence.

Yet this common opinion that mystics are lonely souls wholly absorbed in their vertical relation with God, that their form of religious life represents an opposition to, and an implicit criticism of, the corporate and institutional form of religious life – this is decisively contradicted by history, which shows us, again and again, the great mystics as the loyal children of the great religious institutions, and forces us to admit that here as in other departments of human activity the corporate and the individual life are intimately plaited together. Even those who have broken away from the churches that reared them, have quickly drawn to themselves disciples, and become the centres of new groups. Surely, therefore, it is worth while to examine, if we can, the nature of the connection between these two factors: to ask, on the one hand, what it is that the corporate life and the group-consciousness which it develops give the mystics; on the other, what is the real value of mystics to the corporate life of their Church?

As to the first question: What is it that the corporate life does for the great spiritual genius? – for I think that we may allow the great mystics to be that. First, and most obviously, it gives them a favourable environment. They must have an environment; they must be affected by it. That is a certainty in the case of any living thing; a certainty so obvious that it would hardly be worth stating were it not that those who talk about the mystic craving for solitude – their complete aloofness from human life – seem often to ignore it. The idea of solitude in any complete sense is, of course, an illusion. We are bound, if we live at all, to accept the fact of a living world outside ourselves, to have social relations with something; and it only remains to decide what these relations shall be. The *yogi* or the hermit who retreats to the forest in order to concentrate his mind more utterly upon the quest of God, only exchanges the society of human beings for the society of other living things. If he eliminated all else, the parasites of his own body, the bacterial populations of his alimentary system, would be there to remind him that man cannot live alone. He may shift his position in the web of life, but its strands will enmesh him still. So too, the monk or nun 'buried alive' in the cloister is still living a family life; only it is a family life that is governed by special ideals.

Now it is plainly better for mystics, whose aim is the establishment of special relations with the spiritual order, that the social consciousness in which they are immersed, and from which they are taking colour all the time, should have a spiritual and religious tendency; that the social acts in which they take part should harmonize rather than conflict with their own deep intuition of reality. The difference in degree between that deep intuition and the outward corporate acts – the cult which they thus share, may be enormous: for the cult is an expression of the crowd consciousness, and manifests its spiritual crudity, its innate conservatism, its primitive demands for safety and personal rewards. The inadequacy or unreality of the forms, the low level of the adoration which they evoke, may distress and even disgust mystics. Yet, even so, it is better for them that they should be within a Church than outside it. Compared with this one fact – that they are members of a social group which recognizes spiritual values, and therefore live in an environment permeated by religious concepts – the accuracy in detail of the creed which that group professes, the adequacy of its liturgical acts, is unimportant.

Next, the demands made and restrictions imposed by the community on the individual are good for mystics. Human beings are social right through, in spirit as well as in body and mind. Their most sublime spiritual experiences are themselves social in type. The intercourse of persons with a Person, the merging of their narrow consciousness in a larger consciousness, the achievement of a divine sonship, a spiritual marriage: these are the highest things that they can say concerning their achievement of Divine Reality. And they all entail, not a narrow self-realization, but the breaking-down of barriers, the setting-up of wider relationships. It follows that the merging of self in the common life is an education for that merging of self in the absolute life at which the mystic aims. Such self-mergence, and the training in humility, self-denial, obedience, suppleness, which is involved in it, is held by all ascetic teachers to be essential to the education of the human soul. Union with, and to a certain extent submission to, the Church, to the family – to life, in fact – an attitude of self-giving surrender: this is the best of preparations for that total self-negation of the soul which is involved in union with God, that utter doing-away of the I, the me, and the mine, till it becomes one will and one love with the divine will and love.

On these two counts alone – harmonious environment and salutary discipline – we shall expect, other things being equal, that the richest and most fruitful types of mystical experience will arise within religious institutions rather than outside them, and as a matter of fact this is what we do find. Hindu ascetics have their recognized place in the Hindu system. They have but reached the summit of a pyramid which is firmly based on earth. The Súfí is a good Muslim, and commonly the member of a religious confraternity which imposes a strict rule of life. Christian mystics, too, grow up from the Christian society. Their roots strike deep down into that favouring soil. Though their branches may shoot up to the heavens, and seem to draw thence all the light and heat by which they live, yet they are really fed from below as well as from above. When they refuse to acknowledge this principle, when they abjure the discipline, the authority, the support of the corporate life, and regard themselves as separate individuals, dependent on direct inspiration alone – how quickly they become unbalanced and eccentric, how difficult it is for them to avoid the disease of spiritual megalomania. Refusing the support and discipline of organized religion, they become like poets who refuse to be controlled by the laws of prosody which seem to limit, but really strengthen and beautify, their work.

It is true that right through the history of Christian mysticism there has been a line of insurgent mystics who have made this refusal; whose direct vision of spiritual perfection has brought with it so overwhelming a sense of the imperfection, formalism, unreality, the dreadfulness of religious institutions, that it has forced them into a position of more or less acute revolt from the official Church. So clear has been their own consciousness of the spiritual world that the soul's life and growth, its actual and individual rebirth, have shone out for them as the only things that matter. Hence the dramatization of these things in ceremonial religion, the effort to give spiritual values a concrete form, has seemed to them like a blasphemous parody. Unable to harmonize the inward and the outward – the all-penetrating reality of religion as they understand it, with its crude outward expression in the external cult, where formal acts and intellectual assents so often seem to take the place of inward changes – in the end they solve the problem by repudiating the external and visible Church. This rebel-type, victims of exaggerated individualism, which would make the special experiences of a few the standard for the whole race, has persisted side by side with the law-abiding type, which has preserved, if not always a perfect balance between liberty and obedience, at any rate a more reasonable proportion between them. Often the corruption of the times in which he lived has seemed to the mystic to make such rebellion inevitable. This is particularly true in the case of George Fox, whose ragings were directed far less against organized religion than against unreal religion; and who might, had he lived in fourteenth-century Germany, have found a congenial career as one of the Friends of God. Yet, even so, the careers of these rebels have been on the whole unfruitful, compared with those who remained within the institutional framework and effected their reforms from inside. They seldom quite escape the taint of arrogance. There is apt to be a touch of self-consciousness in their sanctity. We have only to compare the influence exerted by the outstanding figures of the two groups, to realize which type of spiritual life has had the best and most enduring influence on the spiritual history of the race; which, in fact, best stands the pragmatic test.

On the rebel side we have, of course, the leaders of many dead heresies and sects. The Montanists of the second century, with their claim to direct inspiration, their cult of ecstatic phenomena and prophetic speech; the numerous mystical heretics and illuminati of the Middle Ages, often preaching the most extravagant doctrines and always claiming for them divine authority – for instance, the Brethren of the Free Spirit, who claimed the possession of the Holy Ghost as an excuse not only for theological, but also for moral aberrations. Later, there are the Quietists, a particularly poisonous brand of unbalanced contemplatives; and, contemporary with their revolt against Catholic forms and authorities, innumerable mystical revolts against Protestant forms and authorities, the very names of whose originators are now almost forgotten. Amongst these two mighty figures stand up: Jacob Boehme and George Fox. But we must remember as regards Boehme that, although he certainly spoke with great violence against the error of confusing external acceptance of religion with internal adherence to God, 'historical Christians' with 'new men', he never disowned the Lutheran Church within which he was born. On the contrary, it was that Church which persecuted and finally disowned him.

As to that great and strange genius, George Fox, who aimed at nothing less than a world religion of a mystical type, the free and conscious contact of every soul with the Spirit of God, I believe that any unbiased student of his Journal must allow that, enormous as his achievement was, it might have been far greater had his violent sense of vocation, his remarkable spiritual gifts, been disciplined and controlled by the corporate consciousness as expressed in institutional religion. Then some of the energy which he expended in denunciations of steeple-houses might have been employed in healing the disharmony between the visible and invisible Church, helping that vision of the Eternal by which he was possessed to find concrete expression within traditional forms. Here, as elsewhere, the Inner Light would have burned with a better and a truer flame had it submitted to the limitations of a lamp.

I do not suggest that these people, even the most extravagant of them, were not truly spiritual or truly mystical. The sort of criticism which divides mystics into two groups – the orthodox, who are inspired by God, and the heretical, who are inspired by Satan – of course belongs to the dark ages of theology. On the contrary, these rebel-mystics most often possessed – sometimes in a highly developed form – the sharp direct consciousness of the divine life which is the essential quality of the mystic. This was to them the central fact; by comparison with it they judged all other things. What they did *not* possess was the balancing, equivalent consciousness of, and reverence for, corporate human life – that group-personality which is the Church, and its value and authority. They lacked the sense that the whole organism, the whole herd, with all its imperfections, is yet interdependent, and has got to move together, urged from within by its more vivid spirits, not stung from without as if by some enthusiastic spiritual mosquito. To a greater or lesser extent they failed in effect because they tried to be mystical in a non-human instead of a human way, were 'other-worldly' in the bad sense of the word. They have not always remembered that Christ Himself, the supreme pattern of all mystics, lived a balanced life of clear personal vision, unmediated intercourse with God on the one hand, and gentle and patient submission to the corporate consciousness on the other hand. Though severely critical of the unrealities and hypocrisy of current institutionalism, He yet sought to form the group, the 'little flock', in which His ideas should be incorporated within, and not over against, the official Jewish Church; and thus gradually to leaven the whole.

Now put against these vigorous individualists the names of the mystics who have never felt that their passionate correspondences with the eternal order – their clear vision of the adorable perfection of God and the imperfection, languor, and corruption of human beings – need involve a break with the corporate religious life. Observe how these have continued for centuries to be fruitful personalities, often not merely within their own communion, but outside it too; how they have acted as salt, as leaven, permeating and transmuting the general consciousness of the Body of Christ. Often these, too, have been reformers – drastic, unrelenting disturbers of the established order of things. St Bernard, St Hildegarde, St Mechthild, Jacopone da Todi, St Catherine of Siena, Tauler were passionate in their denunciations of slackness, corruption, and disorder. But they made their protests, and brought back the general consciousness to a closer contact with reality, from within, and not from without, the Christian Church. Consider St Bernard and Richard of St Victor, whose writings influenced for centuries the whole of the religious literature of Europe; St Hildegarde, St Gertrude, St Mechthild of Magdeburg, great mystics, good churchwomen but severe denouncers of formalism and unreality; St Francis of Assisi, who removed evangelical poverty from the sphere of notion to the sphere of fact; St Catherine of Siena, who changed Italian politics; St Joan of Arc, who altered European history; the soaring transcendentalism of Ruysbroeck, who was yet content to be a humble parish priest; the great mystical movement of the Friends of God, ardent Catholics and ardent reformers too. Even our own great mystical poets, Donne, Crashaw, Vaughan, Herbert, Traherne, Coventry Patmore and Francis Thompson, were one and all convinced institutionalists. Finally, look at some of the great cloistered mystics, of whom St Teresa and St John of the Cross are types, and see how, though they seem in the eyes of the world to be 'buried alive', they are and remain the ardent centres of a spreading light, which perpetually stimulates and revivifies not only members of their own order or communion, but spiritually sensitive souls outside.

Perhaps it is in those contemplatives who lived within and were obedient to the rule of the great monastic orders, that we can see most easily the nature of the link between the individual soul and the religious group within which it does or should develop, the enormous value to it of tradition, that huge accumulation of tendencies, ideals, systems, wisdom both speculative and practical, which is preserved in the corporate consciousness. Here the influence of the religious family, the rule of life, the ideal held out, the severe education in self-control administered to every novice, can always be traced, conditioning and, I believe, helping and bracing the character of that communion with the Transcendent which the individual mystic enjoys. Babies at birth enter into a civilization prepared for them, and are at once supported, educated, even clothed by a tradition prepared by countless generations of the past. In the same way novices, whose spiritual childhoods begin within a great monastic family, receive – supposing, of course, that the order is true to its ideals – the support and benefits of a tradition evolved during previous generations in response to the needs of other similar souls; and they are so much better off than they would be were they solitaries, or deliberate rebels who refuse to accept the heritage of the past. They find a life beautifully adjusted to their needs, yet which, being greater and older than their own, keeps their rampant individualism in check, nurtures and cultivates their growing spiritual consciousness, and opposes – by its perpetual demands on humility, obedience and unselfishness – the vice of pride which the mystical individualist seldom escapes. Such a mystical consciousness would not necessarily die without the support of this corporate tradition, any more than the baby would necessarily die if it emerged into the conditions of the paleolithic cave instead of into those of the modern nursery. But in both cases the environment would be unfavourable, and the effort required to attain that position into which the child of tradition enters at birth would be an enormous drain upon the powers of the organism.

The instinct of many mystics for a certain measure of solitude is no contradiction of this. The hermits and the anchorites, even such rare and extreme types as St Anthony of Egypt who is said to have lived in perfect solitude for twenty years, did not withdraw from the Christian society, nor did they disown the validity of its external and institutional life. They sought to construct or find within the Christian Church an environment within which their special tendencies could develop in a normal way; and this not merely for themselves, but also for the sake of other souls. Such a period of withdrawal was felt by them to be a necessary condition of their full effectiveness for life. So, too, poets or artists must retreat from their fellows if they are to commune with the eternal loveliness and interpret her to other people: for a total concentration upon reality is the condition under which it is revealed. The Catholic Church has always recognized, and does still in the continued existence of the cloistered orders, the reasonableness of this demand. We do not as a rule say bitter things when people of artistic or speculative genius leave the family group and go to Paris or Oxford in order that their special powers may be educated and become effective for life; nor should we feel resentment because mystical geniuses sometimes feel that the life of the home circle or even the normal life of the community, cannot give the special training which they require. In a few cases the mystics have felt a long period of complete isolation to be necessary to them; but most often they have been accessible to those who really needed them, and helped these all the more because of the long periods of silence in which they listened to the voice of God, too often inaudible for them, as for us, in the general bustle of the world.

Their point of view has been beautifully stated by a young French mystic, Elizabeth de la Trinité, who died a few years ago. 'I want', she says, 'to be all silence, all adoration, that I may penetrate more and more deeply into God; and become so full of Him that I can give Him in my prayers to those poor souls still ignorant of His gift.' She wants to be a channel, a duct, by which the love and power of God, of which she is so strongly conscious, can flow out to other souls. It is not for herself that she is working; it is for the world. Do we not find expressed there both the individual longing and the corporate responsibility of the mystic? And do we not touch here the intimate connection that should exist between the separate life of the great mystic and the corporate life of the Church? On the one hand, the highly organized society, making it possible for contemplatives to develop their special powers in a harmonious environment and preventing the frittering of their energies. On the other, those contemplatives, like special organs developed by the Body of Christ, gaining for the whole community contacts and certitudes, which it could not gain in any other way. News of God can only enter the temporal order through some human consciousness. Is it unreasonable that for so great an office certain individuals should be set apart – within the community, not over against it – and should live in a special way?

As a matter of fact, the Church has gained a thousandfold by her acquiescence in the special vocation of the mystics, for the treasures they won were never kept for themselves but always showered upon her. True, she has not hesitated to scrutinize and control them; sometimes her attitude has seemed to the enthusiasts for liberty to be deliberately obscurantist and tyrannical. Yet, even here – and although in many cases there has clearly been ignorance, injustice, and persecution – mystics gain more than they lose by sub-mission to the collective judgement. Even in their harshest form, discipline and tradition are still priceless for them. First, they school them in the virtue of humility, the very foundation of the Christian character; which is seldom possessed by the spiritual genius who always leads and never submits, and whose triumphant formula, 'God and myself!' too often ends by becoming 'Myself and God!'

> O caritate, vita, ch' ogn' altro amor è morto;
> non vai rompendo legge; nante, l'observe tutto.

said Jacopone da Todi, that natural rebel who deliberately submitted himself to an uncongenial religious authority, and there found perfect freedom.

Next, the solid sense of the community, the mere fact that it always lags behind the more vivid spirits, that the forward-moving shepherd who sees new pastures has got to take account of the slowest sheep – all this is a valuable safeguard against the notorious extravagances of a mysticism unfettered by authority. It is significant that the greatest mystics in all communions have always raised up their voices most earnestly against spiritual license, have been most eager to submit their soaring intuitions to the witness of their Scriptures or the corporate feeling of their Church. They realize the fact that they owe to this Church the huge debt that all individuals owe to the tradition of their art or of their trade. The Church represents a complete spiritual civilization, a conserver of values; were it not for her, every new spiritual genius who arose would have to begin at the beginning, at the Stone Age of the soul. Instead of that, such geniuses find themselves placed within a social order enriched by all the contributions of their great predecessors. The bridges are built; the roads are made and named; their own experiences and discoveries are made more valid, less terrifying, more comprehensible to them, because others have been this way before. Compare the clarity, the sure-footedness as one may say, of Ruysbroeck, of St Catherine of Siena, of St Teresa, with the entanglements, the sense of wandering in beautiful but trackless places, which one feels when reading even Boehme, Fox or Blake; and others are far less coherent than they. Human beings need a convention, a tradition, a limitation, if they are not to waste their creative powers; and this convention the mystics find best and most easily in the forms of the Church to which they belong.

So we see that the corporate life of their Church gives the mystics a good deal. What do they, on their part, give to it?

Those who see the mystics chiefly as people who rebel against, or have no use for, the corporate religious life, and acknowledge no authority but that of their own spiritual intuitions, usually conceive of the mystics' experiences as having value for themselves alone. Mystics cannot, they say, communicate them or teach others to share them. Often, therefore, they are spoken of as useless, selfish, other-worldly: 'lonely souls'. These phrases suggest that those who use them have a very narrow view of usefulness, a very materialistic view of the Body of Christ, and a very unevangelical view of the relative positions of Mary and Martha. As a matter of fact, mystics, instead of being useless, selfish, and other-worldly, are useful, unselfish, and this-worldly. They are creative personalities, consecrated to the great practical business of actualizing the eternal order within the temporal; and although the pursuit of this business brings them hours of exquisite joy it brings them hours of great suffering too – suffering which is gladly and patiently endured. They do it, or try to do it, not because they seek the joy, but solely for love – love of God, love of their fellow human beings – for they are perpetuating in a certain sense the work of Christ, mediating between their brethren and sisters and Divine Reality. Hence, where they are fully developed, they will, as Ruysbroeck tells us, swing like a pendulum between contemplation and action, between adoration of God and service of humanity. In them life has evolved her most powerful spiritual engine; and she uses it not for the next world, but for this world, for the eternalization of the here and now, making it more real and more divine, more fully charged with the grandeur of God.

Often the mystics' special work is done in a positive and obvious fashion which should satisfy the most practical mind, and which is yet wholly actuated by their central intention, that of raising up – as they sometimes say – new children of the eternal goodness, bringing back the corporate life to a closer contact with God. 'My little children, of whom I travail,' says St Paul to his converts. There is a typical mystic speaking of his life's work. Can we call St Francis of Assisi, the most devoted and original of missionaries, a 'lazy contemplative'? Or St Joan of Arc, re-making the consciousness of France by the most active of methods; St Catherine of Siena purifying the Italian Church; St Teresa, regenerating the whole Carmelite Order, and leaving upon it a stamp it has never lost? Or St Catherine of Genoa, the devoted superintendent of a great hospital, who never permitted her hours of ecstatic communion with God to interfere with her duty to the sick?

Taken as a class, the Christian mystics are distinguished by nothing so much as by their heroic and unselfish activities and their varied and innumerable services to the corporate life of the Church. From their ranks have come missionaries, preachers, prophets, social reformers, poets, founders of institutions, servants of the poor and the sick, patient guides and instructors of souls. We sometimes forget that even those known chiefly by the writings they have left behind them have sacrificed to the difficult task of reducing their transcendent experience to words, hours in which – were the popular idea of the mystic a true one – they might have been idly basking in the divine light. But these practical activities, though often great, are only a part of the mystics' contribution to corporate life. If their special claim to communion with the Transcendent be true at all – and this argument is based on the assumption that there is at least some truth in it – then they do really tap a source of vitality higher than that with which other people have contact. In the language of theology, they have not merely 'efficient' but also 'extraordinary' grace, a larger dower of life, directly dependent on their larger, more generous love. This is a claim given weight by their strange triumphs over circumstance, their conquests over ill-fortune, ill-health, oppositions and deprivations of every kind. Not many strong and normal people would willingly face, or indeed endure, the hardships which St Paul, St Francis, St Joan of Arc, St Teresa, gladly and successfully embraced.

This larger and intenser vitality the mystics do not and cannot keep to themselves. They infect with it all with whom they come in contact, kindle the latent fire in them: for the spiritual consciousness is caught, not taught. Under their influence – sometimes from the mere encounter with their personalities – other people begin to live a more real, a more eternal life. Ruysbroeck says that the Spirit of God, when it is truly received into a soul, becomes a spreading light; and history confirms this. Corporate experience of God always begins in a personal experience of God. The rise of Christianity is the classic illustration of this truth; but Hindu and Muslim religious history also declare it. Round each of the great unitive mystics little groups of ardent disciples, of spiritual children, have grown up. This is true both of those who remained within and those who seceded from the official Church – for instance, St Bernard, Eckhart, St Francis, Tauler, Ruysbroeck, St Catherine of Siena, St Catherine of Genoa, St Teresa, Boehme, Fox. Nor did their influence cease with death.

Further, in reckoning up the value of the mystics to the Church as a whole, we sometimes forget the extent to which that Church is indebted to mystic intuition for the actual data upon which her corporate life is based. Christianity, it is true, is fundamentally a historical religion; but it is also a religion of experience, and its very history deals quite as much with the events which attend human intercourse with the Transcendent and Eternal as with concrete and visible happenings in space and time. The New Testament is thick with reports of mystical experiences. The Fourth Gospel and the Epistles of St Paul depend for their whole character on the soaring mystical genius their writers possessed. Had St Paul never been caught up to the third heaven, he would have had a very different outlook on the world, and Christianity would have been a different religion in consequence. Had the Fourth Evangelist never known what it was to feel the sap of the mystic vine flow through him, his words would have lacked their overwhelming certitude. So, too, the liturgies bear the stamp of mystical feeling, and most of the great religious concepts which the Church has gradually added to her store come from the same source.

If we ask ourselves what the history of the Church would be without the history of her mystics, then we begin to see how much of her light and colour emanates from them, how much of her doctrine represents their experience translated into dogmatic form. That communion with – that feeding on – the divine life which she offers to every believer in the Eucharist is the central fact of their existence. From Clement of Alexandria downwards, again and again they appeal to Eucharistic images in order to express what it is that really happens to the soul immersed in contemplative prayer. 'I am the food of the full-grown,' said the voice of God to St Augustine. 'Every time we think with love of the Well-beloved, He is anew our meat and drink,' says Ruysbroeck. So, too, the Church's language concerning new birth, divine sonship, regeneration, union with Christ, and the whole concept of grace regarded as a transcendent life and love perpetually pressing in on humanity – all this is of mystical origin, and represents not the speculations but the concrete experience of the great mystics. They are pushed out, as it were, by the visible Church like tentacles, to explore the unseen world which surrounds her, and drawn back again to her bosom that they may impart to the whole body the more abundant life which they have found. If the unfailing family of the mystics did not thus perpetually push out beyond the protective edges of the organism and bring official Christianity back into direct touch with the highest spiritual values, and so constantly reaffirm the fact – felt and experienced by them – of the intimate correspondence, the regenerating contact of God with the soul, the Church would long ago have fallen victim to that tendency to relapse into the mechanical which dogs all organized groups. Then the resistance that she has sometimes offered to the freshness, novelty and adventurous quality of the mystical impulse, where it has appeared without preparation and sought to correct by its own over-whelming certitude the spiritual conventions of the day, would have become that hopeless inertia that is the precursor of death.

So we may best look upon the great Christian mystics as a special organ developed within the Christian body for a special use. Their peculiar sensibilities, like those which condition artistic genius, are the gates through which messages from the Transcendent come to humanity. They are finding and feeling the Infinite, not for themselves but for us. Their achievement, bridging the gap that lies between the normal mind and the supersensuous world, makes more valid and more actual to us the assumptions upon which external religion is built, vindicating the Church's highest claim, and hence the soul's highest claim – the claim that achievement of eternal life, communion with Ultimate Reality, is possible for the human spirit. And since all human lives interpenetrate, and isolation is impossible save in death, the more we, the social group, are willing to accept the mystics' claim, and receive what they tell us in a spirit of humility instead of a spirit of criticism, the more completely they will be able to share their treasure with us, the more deeply we shall be able to enter into that consciousness which they represent, which they bring in their own person into the human scheme.

This has, of course, been stated far more beautifully and exactly by the Christian Church in her doctrine of the Communion of Saints; and that doctrine, rightly understood, is indeed the key to the connection between the great mystics and the corporate life within which they arise. Were the activities of these more vital spirits wholly hidden from us, wholly silent and supersensual – as they are not – it would be a grossly materialistic and violently un-Christian judgement which concluded from this that their lives were useless save to themselves. How can a life which aims at God be useless, if we believe that achievement of Him is the final destiny and only satisfaction of every soul? It would be an implicit denial of the efficacy of prayer, of the 'prevailing merits' of sanctity and its value to the society that produces it – the power of a great and loving spirit to help, infect and reinforce more languid souls – if we agreed that the life of the most strictly enclosed contemplative was wasted. Christians, who believe that the world was redeemed from within the narrow limits of Palestine, should not thus confuse space with power, or character with the manner of its self-expression. Without the ardent prayers of the mystics, the vivid spiritual life they lead, what would the sum of human spirituality be? How can we tell what we owe to the power which they liberate, the currents which they set up, the contacts which they make? The land they see, and which they report to us, is the land towards which humanity is going. They are like the look-outs upon the cross-trees, assuring us from time to time that we are still on our course. Tear asunder their peculiar power and office from the office of the whole, and you will have on one side a society deprived of the guides which God has raised up for it, and on the other an organ deprived of its real perfection and beauty, because severed from the organism which it was intended to serve.

THE EDUCATION OF THE SPIRIT

✪

THE OLD MYSTICS WERE FOND OF SAYING THAT 'MAN IS a made trinity, like to the unmade Blessed Trinity.' That particular form of words comes to us from Julian of Norwich, but it expresses a thought which we often meet in the spiritual writers of the Middle Ages. Further, these writers were disposed to find in human nature a reflection of the three special characters which theology attributes to the Christian Godhead. They thought that the power of the Father had its image in the physical nature of human beings; the wisdom of the Son in their reason; the creative vigour of the Holy Spirit in their souls. Some also taught that each of these three aspects of humanity corresponded with one aspect of the triune reality of the universe: the physical world of nature, the mental world of idea, the ultimate world of spirit. The sceptic of course would express this differently, and see in it but one more illustration of the fact that human beings always make God in their own image. But without scepticism I think we may explain it thus: that those who have pondered most deeply on the divine nature have most easily found in its richness, and have best understood, just those attributes which are most clearly marked in human nature. Humanity has inevitably been for them a key to God.

These speculations seem at first sight to have little bearing upon the problems of education. But they are in reality intimately connected with it: for their consideration leads as back to the central fact out of which they have arisen – namely, the abiding truth that humanity's deepest exploration of its own nature gives again and again this threefold result, that people feel that their real self-hood and real possibilities are not wholly exhausted by the terms 'body' and 'mind'. They know in their best moments another vivid aspect of their being, as strong as these though often kept below the threshold of their consciousness: the spirit, which informs yet is distinct from both their body and their mind.

Now the question that all serious educationalists are called upon to ask themselves is this: To what extent does that threefold analysis of human personality influence our educational schemes? The object of education is to bring out the best and highest powers of the thing educated. Do we, in our education, even attempt to bring out the best and highest powers of the spirit, as we seek to develop those of the body and the mind?

Children come to us as bundles of physical, mental and spiritual possibilities. They are related to three distinct yet interpenetrating worlds; all accessible to them because they are human, and all offering them endless opportunities of adventure.

> Heaven lies about us in our infancy,
> Shades of the prison-house begin to close
> About the growing boy.

Why should they close? Whose fault is it that they do? Does not the fault lie with the poor and grovelling outlook of those to whom this sensitive, plastic thing is confided? Who select and manipulate the bundle of possibilities offered to them so badly that they often contrive to manufacture a creature ruled by its own physical needs and appetites, its mental and emotional limitations, instead of a free, immortal being, master of its own body and mind. Here is this child, the germ of the future. To a great extent, we can control the way that germ develops; the special characters of the past that it will transmit. We can have a hand in the shaping of the history that is to be when we have gone: for who can doubt that the controlling factor of history is the physical, mental or spiritual character of those races that dominate the world? It is in the interplay, tension, and strife of these three universes that history in the last resort consists.

Now, on the eve of a new era, is it not worthwhile to remind ourselves of this terrific fact? To see whether our plans are so laid as to bring out all the balanced possibilities of the coming human beings, all their latent powers? We recognize the fact that body and mind must be trained whilst still in a plastic state. We are awake to the results of allowing them to atrophy. Where we find individuals with special powers in one of these directions, we aim at their perfect development, at the production of the athlete, scholar, man of action. But it cannot be said that we are equally on the lookout for special qualities of spirit, or that when found, we train them with the same skill and care. Yet if we do not, can we expect to get the very best out of the race? To explore all its potentialities – some, perhaps, still unguessed? We know that children's reactions to life will be determined by the mental furniture with which they are equipped. Their perceptions, their choice from among the welter of possible impressions surrounding them, will depend on the character of their 'apperceiving mass'. Surely then it is our first duty so to equip them that they will be able to lay hold on those intimations of spirit that are woven into the texture of our sensual universe; to lead them into that mood of receptivity in which the beautiful and the significant, the good and the true, stand out for them from the scene of life and hold their interest. A meadow which to one child is merely a possible cricket field, to another is a place of romance and adventure, full of friendly life.

The mischief is that whatever our theoretic beliefs, we do not in practice really regard spirit as the chief element of our being, the chief object of our educational care. Our notions about it are shadowy, and have very little influence on our educational schemes. Were it present to us as a vivid reality, we should surely provide our young people with a reasoned philosophy of life in which it is given its place: something which can provide honest answers to the questions of the awakening intelligence, and withstand the hostile criticism which wrecks so much adolescent faith. For ten parents who study the Montessori system of sense training, how many think of consulting those old specialists who taught how the powers of the spirit may be developed and disciplined and given their true place in human life? How many educationalists realize that prayer, as taught to children, may and should be an exercise which gently develops a whole side of human consciousness that might otherwise be dormant and places it in communication with a real and valid universe awaiting the apprehension of human beings? How many give the subject the same close, skilled attention that they give, say, to Latin grammar on one hand or physical culture on the other? Those subjects, and many more, have emerged from vagueness into clarity because attention, the cutting point of the human will, has been concentrated upon them. Gradually in these departments an ordered world has been made, and the child or young person put in correspondence with that world. We cannot say that the same has been done for the world of spirit. The majority of the 'well-educated' probably pass through life without any knowledge of the science of prayer, with at best the vaguest notions of the hygiene of the soul. Often our religious teachers are themselves no better instructed, and seem unable to offer the growing and hungry spirit any food more heavenly than practical ethics and dogmatic beliefs. Thus a complete world of experience is habitually ignored by us, and one great power of the human trinity allowed to atrophy.

We are just beginning as educators to pay ordered attention to that fringe-world in which sense, intellect, and spirit all have a part: I mean the world of aesthetic apprehension. It cannot be denied that the result has been, for many of the young people now growing up, an immense enlargement and enrichment of life. Look at one of the most striking intellectual characteristics of the last few years: the rapid growth of the taste and need for poetry, the amount of it that is written, the way in which it seems to supply a necessary outlet for young English people in the present day. Look at the mass of verse which was composed, under conditions of utmost horror, on the battlefields – the most pathetic poetry in the world, in which we see the passionate effort of spirit to find adjustment, its assertion of unconquerable power, even in the teeth of this overwhelming manifestation of brute force. There is the power of the future: the spirit of beauty and truth seeking for utterance. There is that quickening spring, bubbling up afresh in every generation and ready, if we will help it to find expression, to transfigure our human life.

There is a common idea that the spiritual life means something pious and mawkish: not very desirable in girls, and most objectionable in boys. It is strange that this notion, which both the Jewish and Christian Scriptures so emphatically contradict, should ever have grown up amongst us. The spirit, says St Paul, is not a spirit of fearfulness; it is 'a spirit of power and love and discipline' – qualities that make for vigour and good character. It is the very source of our energies, both natural and supernatural. The mystics sometimes called it our 'life-giving life', and modern psychologists are beginning to discover that it is, in the most literal sense, our 'health's eternal spring'. People say, 'Come, Holy Spirit' as if it were something foreign to us, yet it comes perpetually in every baby born into the world, for each new human life entering the temporal order implies a new influx or, least, a new manifestation of spirit. But when spirit is thus wedded to mind and body to form human nature, it is submitted to the law governing human nature: the law of freedom. It is ours, to develop or stunt as we please. Its mighty powers are not pressed on an unwilling race, but given us in germ to deal with as we will. Parents are responsible for giving it every opportunity of development, the food, the light, the nurture that all growing things require – in fact, for its education: a great honour, and a great responsibility.

If we are asked wherein such education should consist, I think we must reply that its demands are not satisfied by teaching children any series of religious doctrines divorced from practical experience. They are full of energies demanding expression. Our object is so to train those energies that they attain their full power and right balance; and enable them to set up relations with the spiritual world in which they truly live. The first phase in this education will consist in a definite moral training, which is like the tilling and preparation of the earth in which the spiritual plant is to grow. Regarding the special objects of this training I will take the definition of a great spiritual writer, a definition remarkable for its sanity and moderation: 'If we would discover and know that Kingdom of God which is hidden in us, we must lead a life that is virtuous within, well ordered without, and fulfilled with true charity.' What does that imply? It implies the cultivation of self-control, order and disinterestedness. Order is a quality that all spiritual writers hold in great esteem, for they are far from being the ecstatic, unbalanced and mood-ridden creatures of popular fancy. Now untrained children have all the disorderly ways, the uncontrolled and self-interested instincts of primitive human beings. They are vigorous young animals, reacting promptly and completely to the stimulus of fear or greed. The history of human society, the gradual exchange of licence for law, self-interest for group-interest, spasmodic activity for orderly diligence, must be repeated in them if they are to take their place in that human society. But if we would also prepare in them the way of spirit, the aim of this training must be something higher than that convenient social morality, that spirit of fair play, truth, justice, mutual tolerance, which public school discipline seeks to develop. That morality is relative and utilitarian. The morality in which alone the life of the spirit can flourish is absolute and ideal. It is sought, not because it makes life secure, or promotes the greatest happiness of the greatest number, but for its own sake.

Yet in spite of this, the social order, in the form in which the child comes in contact with it, may be made one of the best instruments for producing those characters demanded by the spiritual life. For what, after all, is the exchanging of self-interest for group-interests but the beginning of love? And what is at the root of the spirit of give and take but humility? See how the approaches to the spiritual kingdom are found in the midst of the common life: what easy opportunity we have of initiating our children into these central virtues of the soul. The spiritual writers tell us that from love and humility all other virtues come, that on the moral side nothing else is required of us. And we, if we train wisely, may lead the young into them so gently and yet so deeply that their instinctive attitude to existence will be that of humbleness and love; and they will be spared the conflict and difficult reformation of those who wake to spiritual realities in later life.

Now humbleness and love, as understood by

spiritual persons, are not passive virtues: they are energetic, and show themselves in mind, will and heart. In the mind, by a constant desirous tendency to, and seeking after, that which is best; in the will by keenness, or, as the mystics would say, by diligence and zeal; in the heart, by an easy suppleness of relation with our fellow human beings – patience, good temper, sympathy, generosity. Plainly the moral character which makes for spirituality is a moral character which also makes for happiness. Suppose, then, that our moral training has been directed towards this eager, supple state of humbleness and love: what special results may we expect as the personality develops? Spiritual writers tell us to expect certain qualities, which are traditionally called the 'seven gifts of the spirit'; and if we study the special nature of these gifts, we see that they are the names of linked characters or powers, which together work an enhancement and clarification of the whole personality – a tuning-up of human nature to fresh levels, a sublimation of its primitive instincts.

The first pair of qualities which are to mark our spiritual humanity are called *godliness* and *fear*. By these are meant that solemn sense of direct relationship with an eternal order, that gravity and awe, which we ought to feel in the presence of the mysteries of the universe; the fear of the Lord, which is the beginning of wisdom. From these grow the gifts called *knowledge*, that is, the power of discerning true from false values, of choosing a good path through the tangled world, and *strength*, the steady central control of the diverse forces of the self: perhaps the gift most needed by our distracted generation. 'Through the gift of spiritual strength', says

Ruysbroeck, 'a man transcends all creaturely things and possesses himself, powerful and free.' This is surely a power which we should desire for the children of the future, and get for them if we can.

We see that the first four gifts of the Spirit will govern the adjustment of human beings to their earthly life; that they will immensely increase the value of their personality in the social order, will clarify their mind and judgement, and confer nobility on their aims. The last three gifts – those called *counsel*, *understanding* and *wisdom* – will govern their intercourse with the spiritual order. By counsel, the spiritual writers mean that inward voice which, as the soul matures, urges us to leave the transitory and seek the eternal: and this not as an act of duty, but as an act of love. When that voice is obeyed, the result is a new spiritual understanding, which, says Ruysbroeck again, may be 'likened to the sunshine, which fills the air with a simple brightness, and lights all forms and shows the distinctions of all colours'. Such a spiritual gift irradiates the whole world with a new splendour, and shows us secrets that we never guessed before. Poets know flashes of it, and from it their power proceeds; for it enables its possessor to behold life truly, that is from the angle of God, not from the angle of human beings.

'Such a one', says Ruysbroeck, 'walks in heaven, and beholds and apprehends the height, the length, the depth, and the breadth, the wisdom and truth, the bounty and unspeakable generosity, which are in God our Lover without number and without limit; for all this is Himself. Then that enlightened man looks down, and beholds himself and all other men and all creatures; and this gift, through the knowledge of truth which is given us in its light, establishes in us a wide-stretching love towards all in common.'

'A wide-stretching love towards all in common.' When we think of this as the ruling character of our future citizens, and so the ruling character of our future world, we begin to see that the education of the spirit may represent a political no less than a transcendental ideal. It alone can bring about that regeneration, working from the heart outwards, of which the prophets of every country have dreamed.

It seems hard to conceive anything beyond this. But there is something. To behold things as they are is not the end: beyond this is that wisdom which comes not with observation, but is the fruit of intimate communion with Reality. Understanding is perception raised to its highest expression: wisdom is intuition raised to its highest expression, and directed towards an absolute objective. It is, so far as we know here, the crown and goal of human development, the perfect fruition of love.

We have considered very briefly the chief possibilities of the human spirit, as they are described by those who have looked most deeply into its secrets. These seers tell us further that this spirit has its definite course to run, its definite consummation: that it emerges within the physical order, grows, spreads, and at last enters into perfect union or communion with the real and spiritual world. How much attention do we pay to this statement, which, if true, is the transcendent fact of human history, the key to the nature of human beings? How much real influence does it have on our hopes and plans for our children? The so-called phenomenon of conversion – the fact that so far nearly all the highest and best examples of the spiritual life have been twice-born types, that they have had to pass through a terrible crisis in which their natural lives were thrown into confusion in order that their spiritual lives might emerge – all this is really a confession of failure on the part of human nature, a proof that the plastic creature has been allowed to harden in the wrong shape. If our growth were rightly directed, the spirit would emerge and flower in all its strength and loveliness, as the physical and mental powers of normal children emerge and flower. What is wrong with education that it fails to achieve this? Partly, I think, that the values at which it aims are too often relative and self-interested, not absolute and disinterested. Its intelligent gaze is fixed too steadily on earthly society, earthly happiness. We encourage our young people to do the best things, but not always from the best motives. We forget the essential link between work and prayer: yet this alone lifts humanity from the position of a busy animal to that of the friend and helper of God. We forget that our duties ought to include the awakening of that clear consciousness of eternity which should be normal in every human being, and without which it is impossible for anyone to grasp the true values and true proportion of life.

From the very beginning, then, we ought to raise the eyes of the young from the contemplation of the earth under their feet to that of the heavens above their heads: to give them absolute values, not utilitarian values, to aim at. There is nothing morbid or sickly in this; it is rather those who do not possess the broader consciousness who are the morbid, the sickly, and the maimed. The hope of the future is wide. We must train our children to a wide stretch of faith, of aim, of imagination, if they are to grasp it and fully enter into the inheritance that awaits them.

How, then, should we begin this most delicate of all tasks, this education of the most sacred and subtle aspect of human nature? We must be careful, for difficulties and dangers crowd the path, cranks lie in wait at every corner. I have spoken of the moral preparation. That is always safe and sure. But there are two other safe ways of approach; the devotional and aesthetic. These two ways are not alternative, but complementary. Art, says Hegel, belongs to the highest sphere of spirit, and is to be placed in respect of its content on the same footing as religion and philosophy; and many others – seers and philosophers – have found in the revelation of beauty an authentic witness to God. But the love and realization of beauty, without reverence and devotion, soon degenerates into mere pleasure. So, too, devotion, unless informed with the spirit of beauty, becomes thin, hard and sterile. But where these two exist together, we find on one hand that the developed apprehension which discovers deep messages in nature, in music, in all the noble rhythms of art, makes the senses themselves into channels of spirit; and this is an apprehension which we can foster and control. And on the other hand the devotional life, rightly understood as a vivid, joyful thing – with that disciplining of the attention and will which is such an important part of it – is the most direct way to an attainment of that simple and natural consciousness of our intangible spiritual environment which all ought to possess, and which the old mystics called by the beautiful name of the 'practice of the Presence of God'.

This linking up of the devotional life with the instinct for beauty and wonder will check its concentration on the more sentimental and anthropomorphic aspects of religion and so discourage that religious emotionalism which wise educationalists rightly condemn. Hence these two ways of approach, merged as they should be into one, can bring the self into that simple kind of contemplation which is a normal birthright of every soul, but of which our defective education deprives so many men and women, who cannot in later life quicken those faculties which have been left undeveloped in youth. As logic is a supreme exercise of the mind, so contemplation is a supreme exercise of the spirit: it represents the full activity of that intuitional faculty which is our medium of contact with absolute truth. Before the inevitable smile appears on the face of the reader, I say at once that I am not suggesting that we should teach young children contemplation; though I am sure that many brought up in a favouring atmosphere naturally practise it long before they know the meaning of the word. But I do suggest that we should bring them up in such a way that their developed spirits might in the end acquire this art, without any more sense of break with the normal than that which is felt by the developed mind when it acquires the art of logic.

What is contemplation? It is attention to the things of the spirit: surely no outlandish or alarming practice, foreign to the general drift of human life. Were we true to our own beliefs, it should rather be our central and supremely natural activity; the way in which we turn to the spiritual world, and pick up the messages it sends to us. That world is always sending us messages of liberation, of hope, and of peace. Are we going to deprive our children of this unmeasured heritage, this extension of life – perhaps the greatest human right of all – or leave their enjoyment of it to some happy chance? We cannot read the wonderful records of the spiritually awakened without a sense of the duty that is laid on us to develop if we can this spiritual consciousness in the generation that is to be.

All great spiritual literature is full of invitations to a newness of life, a great change of direction, which will at last give our human faculties a worthy objective and redeem our consciousness from its present concentration on unreal interests. It urges us perpetually, as a practical counsel, as something which is within human power and has already been achieved by the heroes of the race, to 'put on the new man'; to 'bring to birth the Son of God in the soul'. But humanity as a whole has never responded to that invitation, and therefore its greatest possibilities are still latent. We, the guardians of the future, by furnishing to each emerging consciousness committed to our care such an apperceiving mass as will enable it to discern the messages of reality, may do something to bring those possibilities into manifestation.

The Place of Will, Intellect and Feeling in Prayer

✦

THE PSYCHOLOGY OF RELIGIOUS EXPERIENCE, AS YET SO little understood, has few more important problems to consider than that which concerns the true place and right use of will, intellect, and feeling in prayer. This question, which to some may appear merely academic, really involves the whole problem of the method and proportion in which the various powers and activities of our being may best be used, when they turn from the natural world of concrete things to attend to the so-called 'supernatural' world of spirit – in fact, to God, who is the source and sum of the reality of that world. That problem must be of practical interest to every Christian – more, to every one who believes in the spiritual possibilities of humanity – for it concerns itself with all those responses that are made by human personality to the impact of infinite life. It deals, in Maeterlinck's words, with 'the harshest and most uninhabitable headlands of the Divine "know thyself"', and includes in its span the whole region 'where the psychology of man mingles with the psychology of God'.

In the first place, what do we mean by prayer? Surely just this: that part of our active and conscious life which is deliberately orientated towards, and exclusively responds to, spiritual reality. The being of God, who is that spiritual reality, we believe to be immanent in all things: 'He is not far from each one of us: for in Him we live, and move, and have our being.' In fact, as Christians we must believe this. Therefore in attending to those visible and concrete things, we are in a way attending to that immanent God; and in this sense all honest work is indeed, as the old proverb says, a sort of prayer. But when we speak of prayer as a separate act or activity of the self, we mean more than this. As a rule, we mean, in fact, the other aspect of spiritual experience and communion; in the language of theology, attention to transcendent rather than to immanent Reality. Prayer, says Walter Hilton, in terms whose origin goes back to the Neoplatonists, 'is nothing else but an ascending or getting up of the desire of the heart into God, by withdrawing it from all earthly thoughts' – an ascent, says Ruysbroeck, of the Ladder of Love. In the same spirit William Law defines it as 'the rising of the soul out of the vanity of time into the riches of eternity'. It entails, then, a going up or out from our ordinary circle of earthly interests; a cutting off, so far as we may, of the 'torrent of use and wont', that we may attend to the changeless Reality which that flux too often hides. Prayer stretches out the tentacles of our consciousness not so much towards that divine life which is felt to be enshrined within the striving, changeful world of things, but rather to that 'eternal truth, true love, and loved eternity' wherein the world is felt to be enshrined; and in this act it brings to full circle the activities of the human soul, that

> Swinging-wicket set between
> The Unseen and the Seen.

The whole of human life really consists in a series of balanced responses to this transcendent-immanent Reality; because human beings live under two orders, are at once citizens of eternity and of time. Like a pendulum, their consciousness moves perpetually – or should move if it is healthy – between God and their neighbour, between this world and that. The wholeness, sanity and balance of their existence will entirely depend upon the perfection of their adjustment to this double situation; on the steady alternating beat of their outward swing of adoration, their homeward-turning swing of charity. Now, it is the outward swing that we are to consider: the powers that may be used in it and the best way in which these powers may be employed.

First, we observe that those three capacities or faculties that we have under consideration – the thinking faculty, the feeling faculty and the willing or acting faculty – practically cover all the ways in which the self can react to other selves and other things. From their combination come all the possibilities of self-expression that are open to human beings. In their natural life they need and use all of them. Will they need and use them all in their spiritual life too? Christians, I think, are bound to answer this question in the affirmative. According to Christianity, it is the whole self that is called to turn towards divine Reality – to enter the Kingdom – not some supposed 'spiritual' part thereof. 'Thou hast made us for Thyself,' said Augustine; not, as the Orphic initiate would have said, 'Thou hast made one crumb out of our complex nature for Thyself, and the rest may go on to the rubbish heap.' It is the *whole person* of intellect, of feeling, and of will, which finds its only true objective in the Christian God.

Surely, the real difference that marks out Christianity from all other religions lies just here, in this robust acceptance of humanity in its wholeness, and of life in its completeness, as something which is susceptible of the divine. It demands, and deals with, the whole person, with his or her titanic energies and warring instincts; not, as did the antique mysteries, separating and cultivating some supposed transcendental principle in human beings, to the exclusion of all else. Christians believe in an immanent and incarnate God, who transfuses the whole of the life that He has created, and calls that life in its wholeness to union with Him. If this is so, then *Lex credendi, lex orandi*; our belief should find its fullest expression in our prayer, and that prayer should take up, and turn towards the spiritual order all the powers of our mental, emotional and volitional life. Prayer should be the highest exercise of these powers; for here they are directed to the only adequate object of thought, love and desire. It should, as it were, lift us to the top of our condition, and represent the fullest flowering of our consciousness; for here we breathe the air of the supernal order, and attain according to our measure to that communion with Reality for which we were made.

Prayer so thought of will include, of course, many

different kinds of spiritual work, and also – what is too often forgotten – the priceless gift of spiritual rest. It will include many kinds of intercourse with Reality – adoration, petition, meditation, contemplation – and all the shades and varieties of these which religious writers have named and classified. Just as in the natural order living creatures must feed *and* grow, must suffer *and* enjoy, must get energy from the external world *and* give it back again in creative acts, to live a whole and healthy life, so, too, in the spiritual order. All these things – the giving and the receiving, the work and the rest – should fall within the circle of prayer.

Now, when we do anything consciously and with purpose, the transition from inaction to action unfolds itself in a certain order. First we form a concept of that which we shall do; the idea of it looms up, dimly or distinctly, in the mind. Then, we feel that we want to do it, or must do it. Then we determine that we *will* do it. These phases may follow one another so swiftly that they seem to us to be fused into one; but when we analyse the process which lies behind each conscious act, we find that this is the normal sequence of development. First we think, then we feel, then we will. This little generalization must not be pressed too hard; but it is broadly true, and gives us a starting-point from which to trace out the way in which the three main powers of the self act in prayer. It is practically important, as well as psychologically interesting, to know how they act or should act, as it is practically important to know, at least in outline, the normal operation of our bodily powers. Self-knowledge, said Richard of St Victor, is the beginning of the spiritual life;

and knowledge of one's self – too often identified with knowledge of one's sins – ought to include some slight acquaintance with the machinery we all have at our disposal. This machinery, as we see, falls into three divisions; and the perfection of the work which it does will depend upon the observing of an order in their operation, a due balance between them, without excessive development of one power at the expense of the others.

On the side of spiritual experience and activity, such an excessive and one-sided development often takes place. Where this exaggeration is in the direction of intellect, the theological or philosophical mood dominates all other aspects of religion. Where the purely emotional and instinctive side of the relation of the soul to God is released from the critical action of the intelligence, it often degenerates into an objectionable sentimentality, and may lead to forms of self-indulgence which are only superficially religious. Where the volitional element takes command, unchecked by humble love, an arrogant reliance upon our own powers, a restless determination to do certain hard things, to attain certain results – a sort of supersensual ambition – mars the harmony of the inner life. Any of these exaggerations must mean loss of balance, loss of wholeness; and their presence in the active life reflects back to their presence in the prayerful life, of which outward religion is but the visible sign. I think, therefore, that we ought to regard it as a part of our religious education to study the order in which our faculties should be employed when we turn towards our spiritual inheritance.

Prayer, as a rule – save with those natural or highly trained contemplatives who live always in the prayerful state, tuned up to a perpetual consciousness of spiritual reality – begins, or should begin, with something which we can only call an intellectual act: with thinking of what we are going to do. In saying this, I am not expressing a merely personal opinion. All those great specialists of the spiritual life who have written on this subject are here in agreement. 'When thou goest about to pray,' says Walter Hilton, 'first make and frame betwixt thee and God a full purpose and intention; then begin, and do as well as thou canst.' 'Prayer', says the writer of the *Cloud of Unknowing*, 'may not goodly be gotten in beginners or proficients, without thinking coming before.' All medieval writers on prayer take it as a matter of course that 'meditation' comes before 'orison'; and meditation is simply the art of thinking steadily and methodically about spiritual things. So, too, the most modern psychologists assure us that instinctive emotion does its best work when it acts in harmony with our reasoning powers.

St Teresa, again, insists passionately on the primal need to think about what we are doing when we begin to pray: to 'recollect the mind', call in the scattered thoughts, and concentrate the intellect upon the business in hand. It is, in fact, obvious – once we consider the matter in a practical light – that we must form *some* conception of the supernal intercourse which we are going to attempt, and of the parties to it; though if our prayer be real, that conception will soon be transcended. The sword of the spirit is about to turn in a new direction, away from concrete actualities, towards eternal realities. This change – the greatest of which our consciousness is capable – must be realized as fully as possible by the self whose powers of will and love it will call into play. It seems necessary to insist on this point, because so much is said now, and no doubt rightly said, about the non-intellectual and supremely intuitional nature of the spiritual life; with the result that some people begin to think it their duty to cultivate a kind of pious imbecility. There is a notion in the air that when people turn to God they ought to leave their brains behind. True, they will soon be left behind of necessity if they go far on the road towards that Reality which is above all reason and all knowledge; for spirit in the swiftness of its flight to God quickly overpasses these imperfect instruments. But those whose feet are still firmly planted upon earth gain nothing by anticipating this moment; they will not attain to spiritual intuition by the mere annihilation of their intelligence. We cannot hope to imitate the crystalline simplicity of the saints, a simplicity which is the result, not of any deliberate neglect of reason, but of clearest vision, of intensest trust, of most ardent love – that is, of faith, hope and charity in their most perfect expression, fused together to form a single state of enormous activity. But this is no reason why we should put imbecility, deliberate vagueness, or a silly want of logic in the place of their exquisite simpleness, any more than we should dare to put an unctuous familiarity in the place of their wonderful intimacy, or a cringing demeanour in the place of their matchless humility.

In saying this – in insisting that the reason has a well-marked and necessary place in the mechanism of the soul's approach to God – I am not advocating a religious intellectualism. It is true that our perception of all things, even the most divine, is conditioned by the previous content of our minds: the 'apperceiving mass'. Hence, the more worthy our thoughts about God, the more worthy our apprehensions of Him are likely to be. Yet I know that there is in the most apparently foolish prayer of feeling something warmly human, and therefore effective; something which in its value for life far transcends the consecrated sawdust offered up by devout intellectualism. 'By love', said the old mystic, 'He may be gotten and holden; by thought never.' A whole world of experience separates the simple little church mouse saying her rosary, perhaps without much intelligence yet with a humble and a loving faith, from the bishop who preferred 'Oh, Great First Cause' to 'Our Father' because he thought that it was more in accordance with scientific truth; and few of us will feel much doubt as to the side on which the advantage lies. The advantage must always lie with those 'full true sisters', humility and love - for these are the essential elements of all successful prayer. But surely it is a mistake to suppose that these qualities cannot exist side by side with an active and disciplined intelligence?

Prayer, then, begins by an intellectual adjustment. By thinking of God, or of spiritual reality, earnestly and humbly and to the exclusion of other objects of thought; by deliberately surrendering the mind to spiritual things; by preparing the consciousness for the impact of a new order, the inflow of new life. But, having thought of God, the self, if it stops there, is no more in touch with Him than it was before. It may think as long as it likes, but nothing happens; thought unhelped by feeling always remains exterior to its object. We are brought up short against the fact that the intellect is an essentially static thing: we cannot think our way along the royal road which leads to heaven.

Yet it is a commonplace of spiritual knowledge that, if the state of prayer be established, something does happen; consciousness does somehow travel along that road, the field of perception is shifted, new contacts are made. How is this done? A distinguished religious psychologist has answered, that it is done 'by the synthesis of love and will' – that is to say, by the craving in action which conditions all our essential deeds – and I know no better answer to suggest.

Where the office of thought ends, there the office of will and feeling begins: 'Where intellect must stay without,' says Ruysbroeck, 'these may enter in.' Desire and intention are the most dynamic of our faculties; they do work. They are the true explorers of the Infinite, the instruments of our ascents to God. Reason comes to the foot of the mountain; it is the industrious will urged by the passionate heart which climbs the slope. It is the 'blind intent stretching towards Him,' says the *Cloud of Unknowing*, 'the true lovely will of the heart', which succeeds at last; the tense determination, the effort, the hard work, the definite, eager, humble, outward thrust of the whole personality towards a Reality which is felt rather than known. 'We are nothing else but wills,' said St Augustine. 'The will', said William Law, 'maketh the beginning, the middle, and the end of everything. It is the only workman in nature, and everything is its work.' Experience endorses this emphasis on will and desire as the central facts of our personality, the part of us which is supremely our own. In turning that will and desire towards spiritual reality, we are doing all that we can of ourselves, selecting one out of the sheaf-like tendencies of our complex nature and deliberately concentrating upon it our passion and our power. Also, we are giving consciously, whole-heartedly, with intention, that with which we are free to deal; and self-donation is, we know, an essential part of prayer, as of all true intercourse.

Now, intellect and feeling are not wholly ours to give. Not everyone possesses a rich mental or emotional life; some are naturally stupid, some temperamentally cold. Even those who are greatly endowed with the powers of understanding or of love have not got these powers entirely under their own control. Both feeling and intellect often insist on taking their own line with us. Moreover, they fluctuate from day to day, from hour to hour; they are dependent on many delicate adjustments. Sometimes we are mentally dull, sometimes we are emotionally flat: and this happens more often, perhaps, in regard to spiritual than in regard to merely human affairs. On such occasions it is notoriously useless to try to beat ourselves up to a froth, to make ourselves think more deeply or make ourselves care more intensely. If the worth of a prayerful life depends on the maintenance of a constant high level of feeling or understanding, human beings would be in a parlous case. But, though these often seem to fail people – and with them all the joy of spiritual intercourse fails them too – the regnant will remains. Even when their hearts are cold and their minds are dim, the 'blind intent stretching to God' is still possible to them. 'Our wills are ours, to make them Thine.'

The Kingdom of Heaven, says the Gospel, is taken by violence – that is, by effort, by unfaltering courage – not by cleverness, nor by ecstatic spiritual feelings. The freedom of the City of God is never earned by a mere limp acquiescence in those great currents of the transcendent order which bear life towards its home. The determined fixing of the will upon spiritual reality, and pressing towards that reality steadily and without deflection; this is the very centre of the art of prayer. This is why those splendid psychologists, the medieval writers on prayer, told their pupils to 'mean only God', and not to trouble about anything else; since 'He who has Him has all.' The most theological of thoughts soon becomes inadequate; the most spiritual of emotions is only a fair-weather breeze. Let the ship take advantage of it by all means, but not rely on it. She must be prepared to beat to windward to reach her goal.

In proportion to the strength and sincerity of the will, in fact, so shall be the measure of success in prayer. As the self pushes out towards Reality, so does Reality rush in on it. 'Grace and the will', says one of the greatest of living writers on religion, 'rise and fall together.' 'Grace' is, of course, the theological term for that inflow of spiritual vitality which is the response made by the divine order to the human motions of adoration, supplication, and love; and according to the energy and intensity with which our efforts are made – the degree in which we concentrate our attention upon this high and difficult business of prayer – will be the amount of new life that we receive. The efficacy of prayer, therefore, will be conditioned by the will of the praying self. 'Though it be so, that prayer be not the cause of grace,' says Hilton; 'nevertheless it is a way or means by which grace freely given comes into the soul.' Grace presses in upon life perpetually, and awaits our voluntary appropriation of it. It is accessible to sincere and loyal endeavour, to 'the true lovely will of the heart', and to nothing else.

So much we have said of will. What place have we left for the operation of feeling in prayer? It is not easy to disentangle will and feeling; for in all intense will there is a strong element of emotion – every volitional act has somewhere at the back of it a desire – and in all great and energizing passions there is a pronounced volitional element. The 'synthesis of love and will' is no mere fancy of the psychologist. It is a compound hard to break down in practice. But I think we can say generally that the business of feeling is to inflame the will, to give it intention, gladness, and vividness; to convert it from a dull determination into an eager, impassioned desire. It links up thought with action; effects, in psychological language, the movement of the prayerful self from a mere state of cognition to a state of conation; converts the soul from attention to the transcendent to first-hand adventure within it. 'All thy life now behoveth altogether to stand in desire,' says the author of the *Cloud of Unknowing* to the disciple who has accepted the principle of prayer; and here he is declaring a psychological necessity rather than a religious platitude, for all successful action has its origin in emotion of some kind. Though we choose to imagine that 'pure reason' directs our conduct, in the last resort we always do a thing because of the feeling that we have about it. Not necessarily because we like doing it, but because instinctive feeling of some sort – selfish or unselfish, personal, social, conventional, sacrificial, the disturbing emotion called the sense of duty, or the glorious emotion called the passion of love – is urging us to it. Instinctive emotions, more or less sublimated: love, hatred, ambition, fear, anger, hunger, patriotism, self-interest – these arc the true names of our reasons for doing things.

If this be true of our reactions to the physical world, it is no less true of our intercourse with the spiritual world. The will is moved to seek that intercourse by emotion, by feeling, never by a merely intellectual conviction. In the vigour and totality with which the heroes and heroines of religion give themselves to spiritual interests, and in the powers which they develop, we see the marks of instinctive feeling operating upon the highest levels. By 'a leash of longing', says the *Cloud of Unknowing* again, human beings are led to be the servants of God; not by the faultless deductions of dialectic, but by the mysterious logic of the heart. They are moved most often, perhaps, by an innate unformulated craving for perfection, or by the complementary loathing of imperfection – a love of God, or a hatred of self – by the longing for peace, the miserable sensations of disillusion, of sin, and of unrest, the heart's deep conviction that it needs a changeless object for its love. Or, if by none of these, then by some other emotional stimulus.

A wide range of feeling states – some, it is true, merely self-seeking, but others high and pure – influence the prayerful consciousness; but those which are normal and healthy fall within two groups, one of subjective, the other of objective emotion. The dominant motive of the subjective group is the self's feeling of its own imperfection, helplessness, sinfulness and need, over against the Perfect Reality towards which its prayer is set; a feeling which grows with the growth of the soul's spiritual perceptions and includes all the shaded emotions of penitence and of humility. 'For meekness in itself is naught else but a true knowing and feeling of a man's self as he is.' The objective group of feelings is complementary to this, and is centred on the goodness, beauty, and perfection of that Infinite Reality towards which the soul is stretching itself. Its dominant notes are adoration and love.

Of these two fundamental emotions – humility and love – the first lies at the back of all prayer of confession and petition, and is a necessary check upon the arrogant tendencies of the will. The second is the energizing cause of all adoration: adoration the highest exercise of the human spirit. Prayer, then, on its emotional side should begin in humble contrition and flower in loving adoration. Adoring love – not mere emotional excitement, religious sentimentality or 'spiritual feelings' but the strong, deep love, industrious, courageous and self-giving which fuses all the powers of the self into one single state of enormous intensity: this is the immortal element of prayer. Thought has done all that it may when it has set the scene, prepared the ground, adjusted the mind in the right direction. Will is wanted only whilst there are oppositions to be transcended, difficult things to be done. It represents the soul's effort and struggle to be where it ought to be. But there are levels of attainment in which the will does not seem to exist any more as a separate thing. It is caught in the mighty rhythms of the divine will, merged in it and surrendered to it. Instead of its small personal activity, it forms a part of the great deep action of the whole. In the higher degrees of prayer, in fact, will is transmuted into love. We are reminded of the old story of the phoenix: the active busy will seems to be burned up and utterly destroyed, but living love, strong and immortal, springs from the ashes and the flame. When the reasonable hope and the deliberate wilful faith in which human prayer began are both fulfilled, this heavenly charity goes on to lose itself upon the heights.

Within the normal experience of the ordinary Christian, love should give two things to prayer; ardour and beauty. In their prayer, as it were, human beings swing a censer before the altar of the universe. They may put into the thurible all their thoughts and dreams, all their will and energy. But unless the fire of love is communicated to that incense, nothing will happen; there will be no fragrance and no ascending smoke. These qualities – ardour and beauty – represent two distinct types of feeling, which ought both to find a place in the complete spiritual life, balancing and completing one another. The first is in the highest degree intimate and personal; the second is disinterested and aesthetic.

The intimate and personal aspect of spiritual love has found supreme literary expression in the works of Richard of St Victor, of St Bernard, of Thomas à Kempis, of our own Richard Rolle, Hilton and Julian of Norwich, and many others. We see it in our own day in its purest form in the living mystic who wrote *The Golden Fountain*. Those who discredit it as 'mere religious emotionalism' do so because they utterly mistake its nature, regarding it, apparently, as the spiritual equivalent of the poorest and most foolish, rather than the noblest, most heroic, and least self-seeking, types of human love. 'I find the lark the most wonderful of all birds,' says the author of *The Golden Fountain.'*

> I cannot listen to his rhapsodies without being inspired (no matter what I may be in the midst of doing or saying) to throw up my own love to God. In the soaring insistence of his song and passion I find the only thing in Nature which so suggests the high soaring and rapturous flights of the soul. But I am glad that we surpass the lark in sustaining a far more lengthy and wonderful flight; and that we sing, not downwards to an earthly love, but upwards to a heavenly.

Like real human love, this spiritual passion is poles asunder from every kind of sentimentality. It is profoundly creative, it is self-giving, it does not ask for anything in exchange. Although it is the source of the highest kind of joy – though, as à Kempis says, the true lover 'flies, runs, and rejoices; is free, and cannot be restrained' – it has yet more kinship with suffering than with merely agreeable emotions. This is the feeling state, at once generous and desirous, which most of all enflames the will and makes it active; this it is which gives ardour and reality to humanity's prayers. 'For love is born of God, and cannot rest save in God, above all created things.'

But there is another form of objective emotion besides this intimate and personal passion of love, which ought to play an important part in the life of prayer. I mean that exalted and essentially disinterested type of feeling which expresses itself in pure adoration, and is closely connected with the sense of the beautiful. Surely this, since it represents the fullest expression of one power in our nature – and that a power which is persistently stretched out in the direction of the ideal – should have a part in our communion with the spiritual, as well as with the natural world. The beautiful, says Hegel, is the spiritual making itself known sensuously. It represents, then, a direct message to us from the heart of Reality, ministers to us of more abundant life. Therefore the widening of our horizon which takes place when we turn in prayer to a greater world than that which the senses reveal to us, should bring with it a more poignant vision of loveliness, a more eager passion for beauty as well as for goodness and truth. When St Augustine strove to express the intensity of his regret for wasted years, it was to his neglect of the beauty of God that he went to show the poignancy of his feeling, the immensity of his loss. 'O Beauty so old and so new! too late have I loved thee!'

It needs a special training, I think – a special and deliberate use of our faculties – if we are to avoid this deprivation, and learn, as an integral part of our communion with Reality, to lay hold of the loveliness of the first and only fair. 'I was caught up to Thee by Thy beauty, but dragged back again by my own weight,' says Augustine in another place, and the weight of the soul, he tells us, is its love – the pull of a misplaced desire. All prayer which is primarily the expression of our wants rather than our worship, which places the demand for daily bread before instead of after the hallowing of the Ineffable Name, will have this dragging-back effect.

Now, as the artist's passion for sensuous beauty finds expression in his or her work, and urges them to create beauty as well as they can, so too the soul's passion for spiritual beauty should find expression in its work; that is to say, in its prayer. A work of art, says Hegel again, is as much the work of the Spirit of God as is the beauty of nature; but in art the Holy Spirit works through human consciousness. Therefore human prayer ought to be made as beautiful as possible; for thus it approaches more nearly to the mind of God. It should have dignity as well as intimacy, form as well as colour. More, all those little magic thoughts – those delicate winged fancies, which seem like birds rejoicing in God's sight – these, too, should have their place in it. We find many specimens of them, as it were stuffed and preserved under glass shades, in books of devotion. It is true that their charm and radiance cannot survive this process; the colour now seems crude, the sheen of the plumage is gone. But once these were the living, personal, spontaneous expressions of the love and faith – the inborn poetry – of those from whom they came. Many a liturgical prayer, which now seems to us impersonal and official – foreign to us, perhaps, in its language and thought – will show us, if we have but a little imaginative sympathy, the ardent mood, the exquisite tact, the unforced dignity, of the mind which first composed it; and form a standard by which we may measure our own efforts in this kind.

But the beauty which we seek to incorporate into our spiritual intercourse should not be the dead ceremonious beauty which comes of mere dependence on tradition. It should be the freely upspringing lyric beauty which is rooted in intense personal feeling, the living beauty of a living thing. Nor need we fear the reproach that here we confuse religion with poetry. Poetry ever goes, like the royal banners, before ascending life; therefore people may safely follow its leadership in their prayer, which is – or should be – life in its intensest form. Consider the lilies: those perfect examples of a measured, harmonious, natural and creative life, under a form of utmost loveliness. I cannot help thinking that it is the duty of all Christians to impart something of that flower-like beauty to their prayer; and only feeling of a special kind will do it – that humble yet passionate love of the beautiful, which finds the perfect object of its adoration in God and something of His fairness in all created things. St Francis had it strongly, and certain other of the mystics had it too. In one of his rapturous meditations, Suso, for whom faith and poetry were – as they should be – fused in one, calls the Eternal Wisdom a 'sweet and beautiful wild flower'. He recognized that flowery charm which makes the Gospels fragrant, and is included in that pattern which Christians are called to imitate if they can.

Now, if this quality is to be manifested in human life, it must first be sought and actualized, consciously or unconsciously, in prayer; because it is in the pure, sharp air of the spiritual order that it lives. It must spring up from within outwards, must be the reflection of the soul's communion with 'that Supreme Beauty which containeth in itself all goodness', which was revealed to Angela of Foligno, but which 'she could in no wise describe'. The intellect may, and should, conceive of this Absolute Beauty as well as it can; the will may – and must – be set on the attaining of it. But only by intuitive feeling can we hope to know it, and only by love can we make it our own. The springs of the truest prayer and of the deepest poetry – twin expressions of our outward-going passion for that eternity which is our home – rise very near together in the heart.

THE PHILOSOPHY OF CONTEMPLATION

✦

SUCH A TITLE AS 'THE PHILOSOPHY OF CONTEMPLATION' will seem to many people to beg two questions: one concerning the limitations of philosophy, and the other, the very character of contemplation itself. Yet not really so; for philosophy is the science of Ultimate Reality, and contemplation, if it is genuine, is the art whereby we have communion with that Ultimate Reality. Both then declare that the true meaning of our existence lies beyond us; and both offer to lead us out towards it, by the contrasting routes of vision and of thought. If we took seriously – which of course we do not – Aristotle's definition of man as a contemplative animal, that phrase alone might provide us with a good deal of food for reflection. For this precise thinker did not, with the exclusive mystic and the quietist, call humanity a contemplative spirit. He called humanity an animal, part of the natural order; distinguished from all other animals by what? – the power of contemplation. 'O God, thou art my God: early will I seek Thee.' Alone in the rich jungle of creation, we find human beings wanting to do that. Surely Aristotle was right in picking out this strange desire as the decisive thing about us.

That a scrap of transient life, pinned to this tiny planet and limited by the apprehensions of its imperfect senses and the interpretations of its yet more imperfect mind, should be filled to the brim with a passion for that which lies beyond life – this, even if it only happened once, would present a difficult problem to the determinist. But it happens frequently. Philosophy has not only to make room for the intellectual experiences of a Plato, a Descartes, a Kant, a Hegel. It must also make room for the contemplative experiences of a St Paul, a Plotinus, an Augustine, a Francis, a Teresa; and for the fact that human life only achieves its highest levels under the direct or oblique influence of such personalities as these, and the conviction of spiritual reality and its demands which they alone seem able to convey. They give to our life something otherwise lacking, which we cannot quite get for ourselves. Although it is not a truth which we are fond of, something deep within us insists that Mary has chosen the good, the real, the noble part, and that without her steadfast witness to the perfection she adores, our busy life of becoming would lose all significance.

'The contemplative life is the vision of the principle', says St Gregory. Only human beings are capable of that vision, that discovery of the meaning of life. That is why they are contemplative animals, why it is the good part, and without it there is a cleavage in their lives, the fatal cleavage between idea and act.

Of course contemplation, thus understood, means something far more fundamental than the special kind of devotion which is often called by that name in ascetic books. It means that spiritual realism, that concrete hold on the reality of God, without which religion is hardly more than the beneficent illusion which Freud supposes it to be. It means what von Hügel called our sense of eternal life. 'Every man as such', said William Law, 'has an open gate to God in his soul.' Philosophy merely puts this in its own language, when it says that humanity is capable of the intuition of absolutes. Religion is stating the same thing in lovelier words when it declares that the pure in heart can see God. The link between all these sayings, then, is their insistence that human personality has about it something that is not accounted for by nature, and is not satisfied by nature. We do not belong to the world of succession alone. Deeply immersed though our lives may seem to be in that world of succession, we are yet able to know the Unchanging; and when we forget this, at once those lives are out of shape. 'Ye are of God, little children.' There is within us the seed of absolute life. Therefore in human beings 'most fully human', correctly adjusted to reality, contemplation, the vision of the principle – in other words, spiritual realism – would be the true cause of all action. There should be no cleavage between them.

Here then we have a doctrine that is embedded in the very substance of Christian philosophy; a doctrine which, if we took it seriously, must affect not only our philosophy but our psychology too, and not only these abstract studies, but our whole conduct of life. It would determine our social structures, our educational aims; and movement towards its more perfect actualization would be the only progress worthy of the name. In spite of the so-called revival of mysticism, however, I do not think any one will contend that this doctrine *is* now taken seriously either by philosophy or by religion. We talk and write easily and freely about spiritual values and the spiritual life; but we remain fundamentally utilitarian, even pragmatic, at heart. We want spiritual things to work; and the standard we apply is our miserable little notion of how they ought to work. We always want to know whether they are helpful. Our philosophy and religion are orientated, not towards the awful vision of that principle before which Isaiah saw the seraphim veil their eyes; but merely towards the visible life of man and its needs. We may speak respectfully of Mary, and even study her psychology; but we feel that the really important thing is to encourage Martha to go on getting the lunch. Yet the whole witness of religious history supports St Luke and Aristotle and St Gregory. Understood in the deepest and widest sense, contemplation is the very life blood of religion. It is and has ever been the one thing needful, 'the life of man most fully man'. Be still and *know* that I am God. It cannot be done in any other way. It is true that 'he who runs may read', but he (or she) cannot so easily observe the stars.

So here is something which religious philosophers cannot neglect. It is their duty to heal the conflict between practical life and contemplative life. They must remind our institutional and philanthropic Marthas that the whole sanction for their activities – the only reason why religion exists at all – abides in the fact that men and women do possess a sense of God, of eternal life; that they are contemplative animals. That one fact lies at the root of all creeds, all Churches, all prayer. It is, in fact, one of the key-pieces in the intricate puzzle of our mental and spiritual life. It is a very awkwardly shaped piece for the intellectualist and for the naturalist; but we have got to find its place in the scheme. It is true that we cannot yet make it fit quite neatly. For this, we need much further knowledge of our own many-levelled mental life on one hand, and of the relation between different kinds of knowledge – spiritual, intellectual and aesthetic – on the other hand. But that is no reason for leaving it in the box and ignoring the plain fact that it is one of the most important pieces in the religious complex, and may yet prove the clue to the whole pattern of life. Whatever we choose to call it, it represents the most distinctive and unquenchable of all human passions, the strangest of our endowments; what Plotinus called his sense of the yonder. Thus our whole philosophy of life must be conditioned by the position we give to it; and Christianity, though so much more than a philosophy of life, must have a philosophic scheme, and must make that scheme wide enough and deep enough to accommodate the largest possible number of religious experiences and facts. It is from this point of view that modern philosophies of religion often seem rather thin, tight and academic, terribly inadequate to the profound experiences of the saints, who are after all our chief sources of information, the seers, explorers, artists, great navigators of the ocean of God.

If we do not dismiss them as mere aberrations – and psychology is finding it more and more difficult to do this – the facts of the contemplative life, both in its general diffuse manifestations and its vivid embodiments, involve certain theological and philosophical consequences. The Abbé Bremond, who has devoted two volumes of his great *Histoire Littéraire* to the history and psychology of this subject, speaks without scruple of the 'metaphysic of the saints'. And the true peculiarity of the 'metaphysic of the saints' is the fact that it is controlled by the fruits of contemplation, the certainty of first-hand contact with a spiritual reality that is beyond but not against reason. Therefore a central place in Christian philosophy – indeed, in any really spiritual philosophy – must be left for this strange passion, this peculiar way of knowledge; we cannot avoid our obligations by sending its best products to the convent, and its worst to the asylum. But far more thought and exploration than we have given it yet lies before those who want to harmonize this department of human experience with the rest.

The best modern work on this subject, and on the psychology of religious experience – which is all part of it – suggests that we are at last beginning to move towards a more satisfactory theory of contemplation than any held in the past generation by those who explored it either from the direction of religion or the direction of science; a theory that will interpret tradition in the light of experience and bring us nearer to an understanding of the close relation between religious truth and poetic truth. The most important part of this work has been done in France: by the Abbé Bremond, whose remarkable essay on 'Prayer and Poetry' is now widely known, by the psychologist and theologian Maréchal, and by the philosopher Jacques Maritain. Yet this work is, to a large extent, the recovery and re-statement of doctrine once generally held by spiritual people, and found to be endorsed by their experience.

What then do we mean by contemplation? What is it? When we have considered this, we may see more clearly its place in our view of the human mind and its workings – psychology; and our view of the nature of reality – philosophy. I take it that, in the widest sense, we mean by contemplation the human self's method of stretching out towards truth which lies beyond and above its reason; its communion with a reality which is not given us by the senses, or reached by logical thought. Though it may include the sort of pantheistic reverie sometimes called nature mysticism, real contemplation goes far deeper than this; for its true object is that mysterious something other, the holy and unchanging, which gives meaning to life. If we take our stand by the contemplatives and ask how life seems to them, they will probably say, in their own special language, that it seems to them to be a shifting, intricate half-real process, over against something else, transfused by something else, which is not shifting but is wholly real: something abiding, fully given, prevenient, as theology would say. They will add that for them the visible world derives all its significance from that something else; and that the hours in which they have communion with it are, as St Gregory has it, 'alone the true refreshment of the mind'. At moments, of course – as St Augustine says in 'the flash of a hurried glance' – all, or nearly all, of us, tend to see existence like that. Therefore the contemplative experience is something which we ought not to find it difficult to believe in, even though our own share in it be faint or rare.

When we consider such crumbs of spiritual

experience as have been vouchsafed to us, or look at the general witness of the race, we see that at a certain level of consciousness this sort of apprehension always tends to emerge. There is a pause in our normal useful busy correspondence with the world of use and wont. Another inhabitant comes to the window of the soul and looks with awe and joy upon another landscape, seen because sought and possessed because desired. We all know, that is to say, however badly we express it and however firmly we ignore it, that there is a certain duality in our life: we are not truly one, but truly two. 'In the course of the normal development of man', says Bremond, 'there occur moments in which the discursive reason gives place to a higher activity, imperfectly understood and indeed at first disquieting.' This higher activity – this hidden inhabitant – is intuitive rather than logical in its methods. It knows by communion, not by observation. It cannot give a neat account of its experience: for this experience overflows all categories, defies all explanations, and seems at once self-loss, adventure and perfected love. If we attempt to analyse and pigeon-hole what it gives us, we ruin it at once. But if we accept the evidence it forces on us we have to allow that there are two kinds of real knowledge accessible to human beings. One kind of knowledge is like seeing within a narrow, but sharply focused area. The other kind of knowledge is more like bathing in a fathomless ocean, or breathing an intangible and limitless air. It gives contact and certitude, but not understanding: as breathing or bathing give us certitude about the air and the ocean but no information about their chemical constitution.

Experience as a whole supports this distinction of two quite different capacities in human beings, two different ways of getting two different sets of knowledge. We commonly call one rational, and the other intuitive; one logical and the other poetic; one doctrinal, the other devotional. But these words merely advertise our ignorance. Experience is perpetually hinting that we are far more mysteriously compounded than psychology will yet acknowledge; that we have, as human beings, contact with many levels of reality. In moments of heightened sensitiveness, and especially under the peculiar influence of aesthetic feeling – which still awaits explanation from naturalistic psychology – the psyche loosens its frenzied grip on the obvious world and becomes aware – dimly yet most vividly – of deeper, richer, more universalized realities than the logical reason can reach. But the fullest awakening of this faculty, the most intense, awestruck, and delighted apprehension of absolutes, remains the special prerogative of religion. The peculiar activity of religion which we call in its widest sense prayer, and in its intense form contemplation, is orientated towards this. And wherever people are religious at all, this activity arises and this power is developed with more or less completeness.

Nor are we to think of this reality as less concrete, less rich, more thin and abstract, than the world of our sensory experience. The vision of the principle, however vague and dim our sight, is the vision of absolute plenitude, of all that is. 'Oh! the depth of the riches!' cries St Paul. Such dimness and vagueness as accompany our contact with it, and such contradictions as occur in the descriptive efforts of the mystics, striving to reconcile the extremes of amazement and love, must be attributed to our uncertain touch, our still embryonic spiritual sense. Hence too the tension, and sometimes abnormal mentality, which accompany these adventures upon the very frontiers of the human world. Yet when even the fullest allowance has been made for all this, and for the fact that here 'man's reach must ever exceed his grasp', how impressive is the combined witness of corporate and personal religion to the realistic character of its object, and the breadth and height and depth of that region to which the soul attains in contemplation.

It is strange that the immense importance of these facts has not been more generally realized, for here we lay our finger on the organ of humanity's spiritual knowledge. We use the word 'spiritual' easily and lightly. Yet, if we look at it with detachment, what a queer word it is – what a queer concept it is – for the human animal to have achieved. So useless, indeed meaningless, from the naturalistic point of view; yet entwined in all that we feel most valid, most worth having in life. If we were suddenly asked to define what we meant by the word spiritual, most of us would feel as baffled as St Augustine when he was asked to define time. We too know what it is, until we are asked to describe it. For this is a word that stands for the something other, sought and found in human religion: and, more than this, for a whole range of most real and deep demands and activities, set towards the unchanging and away from the changeful surface of our life. We are constantly compelled to resort to it, in order to find a place for the richest and loveliest developments of that life; for it is just these developments that elude all rational explanation. Heroic sanctity, the instinct of sacrifice, the redemptive power of suffering: these solid facts are quite incompatible with naturalism but entirely harmonious with the world of spiritual reality to which the soul tends in contemplation.

If we put this view of human experience side by side with the scientific view of human experience, what does it require of us, in the way of an enlargement of our conception of the nature of human beings? What adjustments of psychology does it involve? Surely the first question which it forces upon us is this: Is there indeed a faculty, a way of knowledge, in human beings, distinct from the senses and from discursive and conceptual thought, which can give us genuine knowledge of a sort that cannot ever be obtained by means of the senses or of discursive thought? Is the contemplative or poetical consciousness something distinct from ordinary consciousness? When Keats uttered that celebrated, but much misunderstood and rather badly worded aspiration, 'Oh for a life of sensation rather than thought!' was he merely desiring agreeable aesthetic feeling, or was he reaching out to a direct but dimly understood communion with the reality of things? Was he being very superficial, or very profound? However differently they frame or justify their answers, poets, artists and saints agree that he was being very profound. It is their universal testimony that they are not only conscious of a world of reality and beauty shown to them and affecting them. They are also conscious of something else, conveyed by it, or of a distinctive state or condition in themselves; a sort of life, usually latent, which has been stirred to activity. They may describe it in various ways, but all make plain this twofold character of their fullest knowledge.

Stated in its most absolute and provocative form, this means that human beings have not only a natural but a supernatural environment; and not only a supernatural environment, but also a supernatural life: that they already belong to the world of Being as well as the world of Becoming, and under certain conditions can enter here and now into their double heritage. Keats, I think, had discovered and was trying to express this twofold character of human consciousness, for he knew that the secret roots of poetry, as of religion, were planted in the world to which he had access in that generalized awareness, that quiet receptive state which he unfortunately called, because he could find no better term for it, 'sensation rather than thought'. He meant the same thing as that very different poet Matthew Arnold, when he said it was the peculiar privilege of poetry to give us 'a wonderfully full, new, and intimate sense' of contact with the real life of things.

That saying, translated to the theological level, conveys more accurately than many disquisitions on mysticism, the character of contemplation. It gives a full, new, intimate sense of contact with *real* life: in this case, the life of spiritual things. It confers poetic, not scientific, knowledge of God. Not by way of thought, but by way of a willed yet passive receptivity. Not through the logical mind, or the stimulation of the senses, but through something else. So the poet and the contemplative stand side by side – Plotinus and Coleridge, Keats and St John of the Cross – witnessing each in their own manner to an immense tract of human experience which is commonly ignored, or at best indulgently allowed by us. And yet this is the most significant and most characteristic part of human experience; for here human beings disclose their transcendental nature, their inherent power of desiring and discerning eternal life, their passion for absolutes, for God, the supreme object of philosophy and religion.

And this cloud of witnesses requires of psychology that it finds room somehow for the distinction which was first stated by the Platonists, and on which 'spiritual' persons have insisted ever since: the distinction between a 'higher' and a 'lower' self in human beings, that 'somewhat' in them which – however they define it – is capable of eternity, and that natural being they share with the animal world. 'There is a root or depth in thee', says William Law. 'This depth is the unity, the eternity, I had almost said the infinity of thy soul, for it is so infinite that nothing can satisfy it or give it any rest, but the infinity of God.' What we call contemplation is simply the activity of this fundamental hidden self, reserved, silent, but now and then emerging in response to every stimulus which has in it the savour of the Infinite. Even though we never get a clear and steady conception of it – for the soul, as Claudel says, is silent when the mind looks at it – we all know in our own experience that this distinction answers to facts. Martha and Mary do live together in the house of the soul. One is absorbed in multiplicity; the other is gathered into unity. Martha, the extrovert, is busy and loquacious. Mary, the introvert, keeps her secret to herself. One acts, the other adheres. Together they witness to the twofold action of the psyche and the twofold character of that world, both temporal and eternal, in which the psyche is placed. To ignore this duality is to impoverish our view of human nature, and I doubt whether psychology in the true sense is going to establish itself on a firm basis until it consents to recognize this. Nor will practical human life, which is after all psychology expressed in action, achieve harmony and power till it is submitted to the same truth. The integration of prayer and action, tempering and reinforcing each other – depth to balance expansion, and surrender to balance power – this alone can give to human life the richness of reality. Adam must return to contemplation, heal the cleavage in his nature, and accept the full destiny of a creature called to be a link between eternity and time.

I think that a study of method and result in religion, and still more plainly perhaps a study of method and result in creative art – that most fruitful field of research for the religious philosopher – helps us to establish a little more clearly the character and method of this contemplative or transcendental sense. What is the characteristic which confers greatness on a work of art? Surely the fact that in some degree it weaves together two worlds; gives sensuous expression to the fruits of contemplation, and conveys to us a certain savour of the Infinite by means of finite things. The power of conveying ecstasy, said Arthur Machen years ago, is the touchstone and secret of art; and ecstasy is simply a strong name for the release of the transcendental sense, which here communicates its results by means of material given by the senses. Thus, and only thus, can we account for the peculiar stimulus which is given by great art to something in us, which ordinary arguments cannot reach: the solemn thrill of the numinous, removed perhaps at several degrees but still operative, which is felt when we stand in the Cathedral of Chartres, listen to a Beethoven symphony, or read 'The Ancient Mariner'.

Such a work of art, if it is to perform this, its essential office, requires of the artist three things. (1) The contact in his soul's deeps with the reality which lies beyond sense. (2) Its translation into symbolic forms which are accessible to the senses, and with which the rational mind can deal. (3) The energetic will, which selects, moulds and creates from this material a picture, a melody, a poem. The whole artistic and poetic process is a process of incarnation: contemplation issuing in action. Martha and Mary have collaborated in the construction of a bridge along which news from the eternal comes into the sensible world, and enters through this door the field of normal consciousness.

In this respect, the greater part of the literature of religion, and especially all that part which seeks to convey the special experiences of religion, is poetic literature. Many of our muddles and disputes about it would vanish if we would acknowledge this patent truth. Religious literature is trying to convey one thing in terms of another thing and must do so, if it is ever to reach our minds, which, after all, are tuned in to the wavelengths of the visible world. It obeys, in fact, the rules of artistic creation and we shall appreciate it much better if we remember this. In Bremond's words, religious writers are always at work 'turning prayer into poetry', bringing purely spiritual material within reach of our sense-conditioned minds: and the more thoroughly they do this, the better we understand them.

Read without prejudice, such different works as St Augustine's *Confessions*, the *Revelations* of Julian of Norwich or the *Divine Dialogue* of St Catherine of Siena, make this plain to us. All these describe to us, through symbols, a vision of that which in its reality lies far beyond sight and beyond symbol; and they do this by the deliberate and selective exercise of the creative will, weaving a garment in which their vision of God can be clothed. The raw material of this garment is sure to be taken – indeed, can only be taken – from their stock of beliefs, memories, and traditions, and from their visible surroundings. In other words, apperception plays a large part in the creation of spiritual literature.

Thus Ezekiel sees a vision obviously inspired by the masterpieces of Chaldean art that surround him. Yet, borne upon the wings of those living creatures, he truly apprehends the power and the splendour of God. Thus John in Patmos sees a vision for which Ezekiel provides the pictorial form, yet within this familiar symbolism he apprehends the deeper Christian mystery of 'the Lamb that is slain from the foundation of the world'. In each case, then, the image, of which the provenance is so easily traced by us, is merely the carrying medium of something else: something not to be obtained by thinking, but by some other activity of the soul, and which cannot be accounted for by the operations of the surface-mind. We may say indeed of the work of the great religious artist what Professor Lowe says in that illuminating book, *The Road to Xanadu*, of the work of the great poet:

> From the empire of chaos
> a new tract of cosmos has been retrieved;
> a nebula has been compacted – it may be –
> into a star.

Yet in this effort of translation, artists – whether they are
trying to give us aesthetic or religious truth – must
always descend one step from the levels of
contemplation; and in doing so must leave something
behind. They always know this, and it is the tragic
element in their vocation. This is equally true of the
philosopher Plotinus with his strange and almost
stammering hints about the yonder, and his final cry, 'He
who knows this will know what I mean'; of the great
religious genius of Augustine, frustrated and delighted
by that holy joy of which there is nothing he can say; of
the unlettered Angela of Foligno exclaiming, 'Not this!
not this! I blaspheme', as she struggles to put her
overwhelming experience of God into words; of the
learned mystic Tauler, driven beyond all the ordinary
resources of image to speak of 'the Abyss which is
unknown and has no name . . . more beloved than all
that we can know.' Beethoven fighting with the
limitations of sound and rhythm, Dante, at the end of
the *Paradiso*, recognizing the utter inadequacy of the
poet to the final vision of Reality – 'My own wings were
not fitted for this flight' – assure us by their very failure
of a splendour which cannot be revealed. The poet, says
Bremond, is a broken-down mystic. Better perhaps to
say a mediator, an interpreter, who brings us at his or her

own cost the news of eternal life. Men and women who might have had the good part of Mary, but deliberately accept the more homely office of Martha; and dish up some fragments of the heavenly feast for their fellow human beings. The heart of their experience of truth or of beauty, based as it is on an inarticulate though vivid communion – on love rather than thought – remains incommunicable; and they know this.

Nothing is more striking in the literature of contemplation, and of high aesthetic experience, than its steady and unanimous witness to an overplus, an experienced reality, a joy and richness, which can never be conveyed save by allusion. Hence its language must always have a fluid and poetic quality, must suggest more than it ventures to define; for it always points beyond itself, and carries an aura of suggestion. Theology becomes a dead language the moment it forgets this fact. 'Then only', says St Gregory, 'is there truth in what we know concerning God, when we are made sensible that we cannot know anything concerning Him.' 'There is a distance incomparable', says à Kempis, 'between the things men imagine by natural reason and those which illuminated men behold by contemplation.' And St Thomas, yet more strongly: 'Divine things are not named by our intellect as they really are in themselves, for in that way it knows them not.' And Ruysbroeck: 'It is beyond ourselves that we are one with God.' Supra-rational experience: that, however much the intellectualist and utilitarian may dislike it, is at once the paradox and life blood of religion, as it is of creative art. The saints are always telling us of contact with another level of life, which convicts, delights and transfigures them; that 'Clear day of eternity which never changes state into its contrary'. They tell us about it very clumsily, and often by symbols which may or may not be acceptable to us; but they always manage to convey a sense that they have had contact with absolutes.

A Church that has forgotten this, which has abandoned the transcendental temper and fallen from contemplation, has lost the meaning of its own activities. For the whole business of expressive religion – literary, ceremonial and sacramental – is to give something of one thing, in terms of another thing. It has got to give humanity's deepest intuitions of a reality which lies beyond the senses, in such a way that this can combine with the material given by the senses. To put it in strict terms, its business is the symbolic communication of absolutes. It is called upon to bridge the gap between mystical and rational knowledge – move to and fro between contemplation and meditation – and for this it will need all the resources of history, of drama, of liturgical and aesthetic suggestion. Therefore a philosophy of religion which emphasizes the supra-rational character of faith, and remembers that the Church is a society of contemplative animals, can never be – as some suppose – hostile to institutions and external forms. It does not support the shallow notion that there is a necessary contrast between ceremonial and spiritual religion, by any arbitrary limitation of the materials which can be used in this great art-work of the soul. On the contrary it knows that humanity's craving for God and instinct for God require all possible paths of discharge – social, intellectual, ritual, traditional – if the richness of their content is to be expressed.

Such a philosophy as this, I believe, will provide the most promising and solid foundation on which to build that modern apologetic for institutional religion which the Church so badly needs. It is never the genuine mystics who talk about 'dead forms'. They can reach out, through every religious form, to that Eternal Reality which it conveys. For them, every church will be a bridge-church, and all the various experiences of religion graded and partial revelations of the Being of Beings, the one full Reality – God. Conscious of the double nature of their own experience, of the two strands which are present in that incarnate poem we call human life, they are not much troubled by the crude and imperfect means which may be used by religion to convey its ineffable truths; for the most childish and the most sophisticated images may be equally far from representing the holy reality, yet equally able to convey it. The great thing is that the conveyance should take place, and in a way that can reach a wide variety of souls. For this, they know, it must be combined with familiar material which these souls can understand. And that means an amalgam in which there is something of spirit, and also something of sense: something divine and something human too. It means, in fact, incarnation.

If this be true, then it is surely an important function of religious exercises to release and nourish the contemplative sense; and we obtain from this a standard by which to measure their success or failure. The church in which we breathe the very atmosphere of worship – the liturgy that enchants as well as informs – these are doing the work to which external religion is called:

making a bridge between the temporal and the eternal world. This is magnificently taught by that master psychologist St Ignatius, when he makes all the elaborate discipline of the *Spiritual Exercises*, all the moral probing, the deliberate visualizing, and detailed meditation of Scripture, fade away in the end before one thing which he calls 'a contemplation to procure the love of God'.

Leading on from this, it seems worthwhile to ask what this view of the nature of contemplation, this restoration of a belief in the distinctness of Spirit, the double character of human life, is going to do for dogmatic religion. Surely a great deal. For in the first place it calls upon theology to put the transcendent first, to remember that its chief business is always with God and its abiding temper must be adoration. This is already beginning to be realized, and accounts for the enormous influence of such thinkers as Otto and Karl Barth. Though in their struggles to tell some fragments of that which they have known contemplatives often use pantheistic language, their very reaction is a tribute to the otherness and transcendence of God. Further, their steady and awestruck witness to the unsearchableness of the Eternal rebukes the fatuous assumption that we can make a diagram of the divine nature or speak with assurance about 'getting new conceptions' of Him. There is a stern realism about the greatest utterances of the mystics, which shows that the solemn dread which Otto has shown to be a part of all full experience of the *numen* enters into their deepest apprehensions of reality. Were these reports accepted as evidence, they might help to cure the unpleasant and almost impudent familiarity which colours a certain type of popular theological writing.

Secondly, as regards the problems surrounding theological re-statement, a good many difficulties would resolve themselves if we recognized more clearly and less nervously the necessary part which is played by symbol and image in all religious formulas, and the fact that in those formulas we are always dealing with a translation, or rather paraphrase, of a text which we cannot read. For here the Thomist distinction between 'sign' and 'thing' is experienced by the soul in its extreme form.

Thirdly, this view of contemplation might lead to a better estimate of the relation between prayer and faith. For genuine prayer, as all its great initiates have insisted, is the communion of the human spirit with the Spirit of Spirits, a responsive movement towards a prevenient Reality. It is rooted in ontology: an appeal from the successive to the abiding. Even in its crudest forms, then, it is already a sort of contemplation. Its very essence is a mysterious contact, which gives us a certain realistic experience of the Infinite; and by disciplined attention and willed self-abandonment this experience can be deepened, steadied, enhanced. Hence its witness to Reality should be accorded the respectful attention we give to any 'real existent'. The attempts of naturalistic psychology to explain it on subjective lines all break down before any honest and persistent study of its real character and achievements. Therefore what happens to us in this vast and varied world of prayer – the world of our specifically religious experience – will greatly and rightly influence our beliefs. As there can be no valid and realistic doctrine of prayer which does not rest on and involve a doctrine of God; so no doctrine of God can be adequate which does not take account, and even very great account, of the life of prayer. In prayer the soul comes nearest the experience of absolute love: in belief it ascends by means of symbols towards absolute truth. *Lex orandi lex credendi* is true, then, perhaps in a far more actual sense than those who first made that axiom supposed. It is only by a fuller entrance into this world of prayer that we obtain a standard by which to interpret religious history which tells us of other contacts, other experiences of eternal life. Here alone we can develop the spiritual sympathy, the peculiar sensitiveness, which is essential to the understanding of spiritual truth; for religion, like beauty, cannot be experienced in cold blood.

Dogmatic theology is largely concerned with truth as seen from within the house of prayer and contemplation. For here, within the house, though the lighting is dim and some of the furniture is clumsy and much that we vaguely perceive is beyond our comprehension, we do at least realize the use of those pipes and chimney-pots which looked so queer and disconcerting from outside. Our difficulty in giving living content to our religious formulas, the dreadful sense of unreality which clings to many of the definitions of faith, arise very largely from the fact that we are thus viewing from the outside that which can only disclose its meaning when seen from within. Thus, for instance, the problems of Christology entirely change their form and colour when they are viewed within this atmosphere, gaining a new mystery, beauty and depth.

Along these lines, perhaps, the modern world may be brought to realize that religion is not to be justified by the improvements it may effect in this world, but by the news that it gives of another world. It is true that when this news – this metaphysical reality – is brought into human life and becomes dominant, all our reactions to the physical are profoundly modified. The more eternal life permeates our mentality, the more deep and rich becomes our interpretation of temporal life, and the higher our standard of responsibility rises. And were the fusion between contemplation and action complete, the Kingdom of God – which is already within, in the ground of our personality – would be manifest in space and time. But the moment religion begins to place these practical advantages in the foreground and depart from disinterested adoration, it has cut itself off from its sources of power.

Finally, if we accept – of course under due safe-guards – the central experiences of contemplatives, their claim to a certain freely given contact with absolutes, as giving us real news about the universe; what effect will this have upon pure philosophy?

First, it is wholly incompatible not only with any mechanistic theory of reality and any form of subjective idealism but also with those sloppy levelling down types of monism, which seem to offer an easy (far too easy) reconciliation of religion and science and form the backbone of much popular apologetic. Next, as against naturalism, it presses upon us a conviction of the concrete reality and distinctness of the supernatural. For though the psychological accidents that often accompany contemplation may be very neatly explained by physiology or even biochemistry, both the essential experience and its transforming results are still left over. These, if we take them seriously, force us to admit the existence of a knowledge *wholly other* in method and content than our knowledge of the natural world: a knowledge which in its wholeness impresses itself on the whole self, in so far as that self turns towards it with a receptive attention. For the contemplative experience bears its own witness to the character of God correcting the modern emphasis on visible nature as the capital scene of His self-disclosure to man. It leads the self into a level of life other than that of nature, and shows it the rich and mysterious web of existence in spiritual regard.

Hence the genuine knowledge of divine immanence that grows with the deepening of humanity's prayer is always the knowledge of a divine otherness; and the constantly heard invitations to seek and find God in nature – that is to say in the physical scene, or rather our imperfect and ever-changing apprehension of the physical scene – may result in actual damage to the deepest interests of religion, if it is allowed to obscure the primacy of those revelations of an unchanging reality made only in that deep communion where the spirit 'seeks God in her ground'. For then something enters human experience from beyond the range of sensible perception and intellectual analysis, requiring from us the acknowledgement that we, though immersed in the temporal, do live and have our being within the mysterious precincts of an eternal world, supra-sensible indeed but not wholly unknowable. Whatever guess we make about the ultimate nature of reality, it must leave room for the fact that the fullest human experience always has this dual character. That discovery of one world in and through another world, which is the essence of sacramentalism, speaks to us as it does just because we too are double: really things of spirit and really things of sense. I do not wish to use the controversial word dualism, but only to point to some facts of experience which the monist never seems to take sufficiently seriously.

Last, when stripped of the symbolic language in which it is always conveyed to us, philosophy finds that the experience of contemplation is at bottom an experience of value – of the quality, not the quantity, of Ultimate Truth. We obtain from genuine mystical literature a united witness to the splendour, the joy, the inherent goodness of this Ultimate and of its immanence, its insistent living pressure on the still undeveloped, half-grown consciousness of humanity. Because of that experience, philosophy – and especially the philosophy of religion – cannot rest content with any theory of life and knowledge which is not sufficiently wide and deep to include and interpret St Thomas Aquinas as well as the last findings of naturalistic psychology. Not only that St Thomas who so patiently classified and explained the gropings of the intellect towards God; but the far greater and more significant St Thomas who quietly put away his pen and parchment saying: 'I have seen too much, I can write no more.' The St Thomas who had passed from knowledge to wisdom, and from reason to contemplation.

SPIRITUAL LIFE

✦

'SPIRITUAL LIFE' IS A VERY ELASTIC PHRASE WHICH CAN either be made to mean the most hazy religiosity and most objectionable forms of uplift, or be limited to the most exclusive types of contemplation. Yet surely we should not mean by it any of these things, but something which for most of us is much more actual, more concrete; indeed, an essential constituent of all human life worthy of the name. I am not proposing to talk about mystics or anyone who has rare and peculiar religious experience, but simply about ourselves, normal people living the natural social and intellectual life of our time. If we know much about ourselves, I think we must agree that there is something in us which, in spite of all the efforts of a materialistic psychology, is not accounted for either by the requirements of natural life or those of social life, and which cannot altogether be brought within the boundaries of the intellectual and rational life. Though as it develops this 'something' will penetrate and deeply affect all these levels of our existence, we recognize that it is distinct from them. It is an element which is perhaps usually dormant; yet is sometimes able to give us strange joys, and sometimes strange discomforts. It points beyond our visible environment to something else; to a reality which transcends the time-series, and yet to which we, because of the existence of this quality in us, are somehow akin.

By talking of 'spirit' or 'spiritual life' – terms more allusive than exact – we do not make these facts less mysterious. But we do make it possible to think about them, and consider what they must involve for our view of the nature of reality; what light they cast on the nature of human beings; and finally how this quality which we call 'spiritual life' calls us, as spirits, to act. In other words, we are brought up against the three primary data of religion: God, the soul, and the relation between God and the soul. Those three points, I think, cover the main aspects of humanity's life as spirit. They become, as people grow in spiritual awareness and responsiveness, more and more actual to them, and more and more fully incorporated in their experience. And they are all three represented in the life of prayer; which, taken in the widest sense, is the peculiar spiritual activity of human beings. By prayer, of course, I do not merely mean primitive prayer – the clamour of the childish creature for help, relief or gifts from beyond – though this survives in us, as all our primitive and instinctive life still survives. I mean the developed prayer of the soul which has taken its Godward life, its link with the Eternal, seriously; has knocked and had a door opened on to a fresh range of experience. Such prayer as that is just as much a human fact as great achievement in music or poetry and must be taken into account in estimating the possibilities of human life.

We begin then with this fact of something in us

which points beyond physical life, however complete that physical life may be, and suggests – perhaps in most of us very faintly and occasionally, but in some with a decisive authority – that somehow we are borderland creatures. As human beings, we stand between an order of things which we know very well, to which most of us are more or less adapted and in which we can easily immerse ourselves, and another order, of which we do not know much but which, if we respond to it and develop a certain suppleness in respect of it, can gradually become the most important factor in our lives. We might sum this up by saying that there is in us a fringe-region where human personality ceases to be merely natural and takes up characteristics from another order, yet without losing concrete hold upon what we call natural life. It is in this fringe-region of our being that religion is born. It points to the fact that we need to be met and completed by an order of being, a reality, that lies beyond us. We are in the making; and such significance as we have is the significance of a still unfinished thing.

Of course, in the pitter-patter of temporal existence it is very easy to lose all sense of this otherness and incompleteness of life, this mysterious quality in human nature. Attention, will and intelligence have all been trained in response to the physical and turn most easily that way. We live too in a time of immense corporate self-consciousness. Modern literature, with its perpetual preoccupation with the details of our emotional and sexual relationships, reflects this. Universals, and our relation to universals, are neglected. Yet without some recognition of our relation to reality, we are only half-human; and if we are alert, we cannot entirely miss all consciousness of the presence and pressure of that reality, that eternal order, however we may represent it to ourselves. The strange little golden intimations of beauty and holiness that flash up through life, however they come, do present a fundamental problem to us. Are these intimations of reality in its most precious aspect, the faint beginnings of an experience, a development of life, towards which we can move; or are they mere will-o'-the-wisps? Shall we trust them and give them priority, or regard them with the curiosity that borders on contempt?

In other words, is reality spiritual? Is the only concrete reality God, as the mystics have always declared? And is that richly real and living God present to and pressing upon His whole creation, especially His spiritual creation, or is this merely a pious idea? Are humanity's small spiritual experiences testimonies to a vast truth, which in its wholeness lies far beyond us, or not? We have to choose between these alternatives; and the choice will settle the character of our religion and philosophy, and will also colour the whole texture of existence, the way we do our daily jobs.

We assume that the first alternative is the true one; that human beings are created spirits still in the making, and can experience a communion with that living God, Spirit of all spirits, who is the Reality of the universe. What we call our religious experiences, are genuine if fragmentary glimpses of this Divine Reality. That belief, of course, lies at the very heart of real Christian theism. In thinking about it, we are not moving off to some peculiar or specialized mystical religion; we are exploring the treasures of our common faith. And the first point that comes out of it for us, I think, is the distinctness and independence of God and of eternal life as realities so wholly other than the natural order and the natural creature that they must be given us from beyond ourselves. A great deal of modern Christianity, especially that type which is anxious to come to terms with theories of emergent evolution and other forms of immanentism, seems to me to be poisoned by a kind of spiritual self-sufficiency which tends to blur this fundamental and humbling distinction between the creature and God, and between the natural and spiritual life. It perpetually suggests that all we have to do is to grow, develop, unpack our own spiritual suitcases; that nothing need be given us or done to us from beyond.

Were the fullest possible development of their natural resources the real end of human beings, this might be true enough. But all the giants of the spiritual life are penetrated through and through by the conviction that this is not the goal of human existence, that something must be given, or done to them, from the eternal world over-against us, without which humanity can never be complete. They feel, however variously they express it, that for us in our strange borderland situation there must be two orders, two levels of reality, two mingled lives, to both of which we are required to respond – the natural and the spiritual, nature and grace, life towards others and life towards God – and that the life of spirit of which we are capable must come to us, before we can go to it. It is surely the true instinct of religion which fills the liturgy with references to something which must be given or poured out on us. 'Pour down on us the continual dew of Thy blessing' – 'Pour into our hearts such love towards Thee' – 'Without Thee we are not able to please Thee.' All summed up in the wonderful prayer of St Augustine: 'Give what Thou dost demand; and then, demand what Thou wilt.'

So I suppose, from the human point of view, a spiritual life is a life which is controlled by a gradually developing sense of the eternal, of God and His transcendent reality; an increasing capacity for Him, so that our relation to God becomes the chief thing about us, exceeding and also conditioning our relationship with each other. So here the first and second points which we were to consider – what we mean by a spiritual life, and what a spiritual life involves for us – seem to melt into one other. Indeed, it is almost impossible to consider them separately. For what it means for us is surely this: that we are meant, beyond the physical, to contribute to, indeed collaborate in, God's spiritual creation; to be the willing and vigorous tools and channels of His action in time. That is the spiritual life of humanity at its fullest development, the life of all great personalities: saints, artists, explorers, servants of science. It is a life infinite in its variety of expression, but marked by a certain deep eternal quality, a disinterested zest for perfection, in all its temporal acts.

When we come to make the personal application of these ideas, this view of the relation of our fluid, half-made personalities to God, and ask how, as individuals, we are called to act – and that is the third of the questions with which we started – we see that just in so

far as this view of human life is realistic, it lays on each
of us a great and a distinct obligation. Though the life of
the Spirit comes from God, the ocean of our being, we
have to do something about it. Utter dependence on
God must be balanced by courageous initiative. Each of
us has a double relationship and is required to develop a
double correspondence. First with the Divine Creative
Spirit who penetrates and supports our spirits; and
secondly with the universe of souls, which is enlaced
with us in one vast web of being – whether our
immediate neighbours of the Christian family who form
with us part of the Mystical Body of Christ, or the more
widespread corporation of all the children of God, of
which this perhaps forms the nucleus.

For those who see life thus, sustained and fed by a
present God, and who can say with St Augustine 'I
should not exist wert not Thou already with me', the
idea of mere self-determination, self-expression as an
end in itself, becomes ridiculous. Further than this, the
notion of souls, persons, as separate ring-fenced units, is
also seen to be impossible. In many ways that are
perceptible, and many others so subtle as to be
imperceptible, we penetrate and affect one another. The
mysterious thing called influence points to our far-
reaching power and responsibility and the plastic
character of the human self. Because of this plasticity,
this interpenetration of spirits, those who have
developed their capacity for God, have learnt, as St John
of the Cross says, how to direct their wills vigorously
towards Him, can and do become channels along which
His life and power can secretly but genuinely transform
some bit of life. Devotion by itself has little value, may

even by itself be a form of self-indulgence, unless it issues in some costly and self-giving action of this kind.

The spiritual life of any individual, therefore, has to be extended both vertically to God and horizontally to other souls; and the more it grows in both directions, the less merely individual and therefore the more truly personal it will be. It is, in the truest sense, in humanity that we grow by this incorporation of the spiritual and temporal, the deeps and the surface of life; getting more not less rich, various and supple in our living out of existence. Seen from the spiritual angle, Christian selves are simply parts of that vast organism, the Church Invisible, which is called upon to incarnate the divine life in history, and bring eternity into time. Each one of us has his or her own place in this scheme, and each is required to fulfil a particular bit of that plan by which the human world is being slowly lifted Godward, and the Kingdom of God is brought in. This double action – interior and ever-deepening communion with God and, because of it, ever-widening outgoing towards the world as tools and channels of God, the balanced life of faith and works, surrender and activity – must always involve a certain tension between the two movements. Nor, as St Paul saw, should we expect the double movement to be produced quite perfectly in any one individual, not even in the saints. The body has many members, some of them a very funny shape but each with their own job. The person of prayer and the person of action balance and complete one another. Every genuine vocation must play its part in this transformation in God of the whole complex life of humanity.

Humans are the only created beings of which we

have knowledge, who are aware of this call, this need of putting themselves in one way or another at the disposal of Creative Spirit; and this characteristic, even though it is only occasionally developed to the full in human nature, assures us that there is in that nature a certain kinship with God. So every human soul without exception, because of its mysterious affinity with God, and yet its imperfect status, its unlikeness from God, is called to undertake a growth and a transformation that will make of it a channel of the divine energy and will. Such a statement as this, of course, is not to be narrowed down and limited to that which we call the 'religious' life. On the contrary it affirms the religious character of all full life. For it means a kind of self-oblivious faithfulness in response to all the various demands of circumstance, the carrying through of everything to which one sets one's hand, which is rooted in a deep – though not necessarily emotional – loyalty to the interests of God. That conception expands our idea of the religious life far beyond the devotional life, till there is room in it for all the multiple activities of human beings in so far as they are prosecuted in, for, and with the Fact of all facts, God-Reality.

I need not point out that for Christians the incarnation – the entrance of God into history – and its extension in the Church bring together these two movements in the soul and in the human complex and start a vast process, to which every awakened soul which rises above self-interest has some contribution to make. As we become spiritually sensitive, and more alert in our response to experience, I think we sometimes get a glimpse of that deep creative action by which we are being brought into this new order of being, more and more transformed into the agents of spirit and able to play our part in the great human undertaking of bringing the whole world nearer to the intention of God. We then perceive the friction of circumstance, the hard and soft of life, personal contacts and opportunities, love and pain and dreariness, to be penetrated and used by a Living Influence, which is making by this means both changes and positive additions to our human nature – softening, deepening, enriching and moulding the raw material of temperament into something nearer the Artist's design.

Next, let us look for a moment at prayer as the special reflection and expression of this relation of God and soul of which we have been thinking. Prayer is, if not the guarantee, at least a mighty witness to the reality of the spiritual life. If we were merely clever animals, had no kinship with God, we could not pray: no communion between Him and us would be possible. Prayer, in its three great forms of worship, communion and intercession, is after all a purely spiritual activity, an acknowledgement of the supreme reality and power of the spiritual life in human beings. As St Thomas says, it is a 'marvellous intercourse between Infinite and finite, God and the soul'.

If the first term of the spiritual life is recognition in some way or other of the splendour and reality of God, the first mood of prayer – the ground from which all the rest must grow – is certainly worship, awe, adoration; delight in that holy reality for its own sake. This truth has lately returned to the foreground of religious thought; and there is little need to insist on it afresh.

Religion, as von Hügel loved to say, *is* adoration: humanity's humble acknowledgement of the transcendent, the fact of God – the awestruck realism of the seraphs in Isaiah's vision – the meek and loving sense of mystery which enlarges the soul's horizon and puts us in our own place. Prayer, which is so much more a state and condition of soul than a distinct act, begins there, in the lifting of the eyes of the little creature to the living God, or perhaps to the symbol through which the living God reveals Himself to the soul.

It is mainly because we are unaccustomed to a spiritual outlook which is centred on the infinite mystery of God and not merely on ourselves and our own needs and desires, that we so easily become confused by the changes and chances of experience. And for modern people, confronted as we all are by a swiftly changing physical and mental universe sweeping away as it must many old symbolic constructions but giving in their place a fresh and humbling sense of the height and depth and breadth of creation and our own small place in it, it is surely imperative to establish and feed this adoring sense of the unchanging reality of God. It is easy, so long as the emphasis lies on us and our immediate interests, to be baffled and depressed by a sense of our own futility. Our whole life may seem to be penned down to attending to the horrid little tea-shop in the valley, yet this and every other vocation is ennobled if we find time each day to lift our eyes to the everlasting snows. I think we might make far greater efforts than we do to get this adoring remembrance of the reality of God, who alone gives our work significance, woven into our everyday lives. There is no more certain method of evicting pettiness, self-occupation and unrest, those deadly enemies of the spiritual self.

It is within this penetrating sense of God present yet transcendent, which at once both braces and humbles us, that the second stage of prayer – a personal self-giving that culminates in a personal communion – emerges and grows. Here we have the personal response and relationship of the self to that God who has evoked our worship. Adoration, as it more deeply possesses us, inevitably leads on to self-offering, for every advance in prayer is really an advance in love. 'I ask not for thy gifts but for thyself', says the divine voice to Thomas à Kempis. There is something in all of us which knows that to be true. True, because of the fact of human freedom: because human beings have the awful power of saying Yes or No to God and His purposes, linking up our separate actions with the great divine action or pursuing a self-centred or earth-centred course. This is the heart of practical religion, and can be tested on the common stuff of our daily lives. It is this fact of freedom which makes sacrifice, with its elements of personal cost and confident approach and its completion in communion, the most perfect symbol of the soul's intimate and personal approach to God. If worship is the lifting up towards the Infinite of the eyes of faith, self-offering is the prayer of hope: the small and fugitive creature giving itself, its thoughts, deeds, desires in entire confidence to the mysterious purposes of eternal life. It is summed up in the great prayer of St Ignatius: 'Take Lord, and receive!'

But as the realistic sense of God in Himself which

is the basis of adoration leads on to a realistic personal relationship with Him in self-offering and communion, so from this self-offering and communion there develops that full and massive type of prayer in which spiritual power is developed and human creatures become fellow workers with the Spirit, tools and channels through which God's creative work is done. That is the life of charity, the life of friendship with God for which we were made. Growth in spiritual personality means growth in charity. And charity – energetic love of God, and of all people in God – operating in the world of prayer, is the live wire along which the power of God, indwelling our finite spirits, can and does act on other souls and other things, rescuing, healing, giving support and light. That, of course, is real intercession, which is gravely misunderstood by us if we think of it mainly in terms of asking God to grant particular needs and desires. Such secret intercessory prayer ought to penetrate and accompany all our active work if it is really to be turned to the purposes of God. It is the supreme expression of the spiritual life on earth: moving from God to human beings, through us, because we have ceased to be self-centred units but are woven into the great fabric of praying souls, the 'mystical body' through which the work of Christ on earth goes on being done.

We talk about prayer thus by means of symbols; but as a matter of fact we cannot really rationalize it without impoverishing it. It leads us into the world of mystery where the Creative Spirit operates, in ways beyond and above all we can conceive, yet along paths which touch and can transform at every point our humble daily lives and activities. Thus prayer, as the heart of our spiritual life – our Godward response and striving – is seen to be something which far exceeds devotional exercises and is and must be present in all disinterested striving for perfection, for goodness, for truth and beauty, or for the betterment of the children of God. For it means the increasing dedication and possession of all our faculties by Him, the whole drive of our active will subdued to His design, penetrated by His life and used for His ends.

And last, coming down to ourselves, how does all this work out in the ordinary Christian life? It works out, I think, as a gradual growth in the soul's adherence to God and co-operation with God, achieved by three chief means: 1. Discipline, mental, moral and devotional. 2. Symbolic and sacramental acts. 3. Ever-renewed and ever more perfect dedication of the will; death to self. This point, of course, is incomparably the most important. The others have their chief meaning in the fact that they contribute to and support it.

Discipline. This includes the gradual training of our faculties to attend to God, by the regular practice of meditation and recollected vocal prayer. Also such moral drill as shall conduce to the conquest of the instinctive nature, the triumph of what traditional asceticism calls the 'superior faculties of the soul' or, in plain English, getting ourselves thoroughly in hand. At least, in the experience of most souls, this will involve a certain moderate amount of real asceticism, a painful effort to mortify faults of character, especially those which are ramifications of self-love, and a humble submission to some elementary education in devotional routine. Under this head we get an ordered rule of life, voluntary self-denials and a careful detachment of the emotions from all overwhelming attractions which compete with God. Acceptance of the general methods and regulations of the Church also comes in here, as the first stage in that very essential process, the socializing and incorporation of the individual life of prayer so that it may find its place, and make its contribution to the total life of the Mystical Body of Christ. None of this is actual prayer; but all of it, in various degrees, must enter into the preparation of the self for prayer.

Next, *symbolic acts*. Even if we can dare to say that there is such a thing as an absolute and purely spiritual communication of God with the soul (and such a mystically inclined theologian as von Hügel thought that we could not say this), such absolute communications are at best rare and unpredictable flashes and, even where they seem to us to happen, are confined to the highest ranges of spiritual experience. They could never form its substance; and it would be an intolerable arrogance on our part – a departure from creatureliness bringing its own punishment with it – if we planned our inner life on such lines. We are sense-conditioned, and must use the senses in our approach to God, accepting the humbling truth that His absolute being is unknowable and can only be apprehended by us under symbols and incarnational veils. This of course is both Christianity and common sense.

But as well as this, we have to acknowledge that the real nature of His work within the soul is also unknowable by us. When we enter the phase of suffering, this truth becomes specially clear. Only by its transforming action within the mental or volitional life, purifying, illuminating, stirring to fervour or compelling to sacrifice, can we recognize the creative working of God. And even these inward experiences and acts, vital as they are for us, are still only symbolic in their conveyance of God. Récéjac's celebrated definition of mysticism as 'the tendency to approach the Absolute morally and by means of symbols' covers, when we properly understand it, the whole spiritual life of human beings, for the ground of the soul where His Spirit and our freedom meet is beyond the reach of our direct perceptions. There is therefore no realistic religion for the human creature which is not expressed in symbolic acts. We cannot cut our world into two mutually exclusive parts and try to achieve the Infinite by a rejection of the finite. And when and if those more profound and really mystical depths of prayer are reached where we seem indeed to be subdued to a presence and action which has no image, and of which we can say nothing at all – when the eternal background has become the eternal environment and we are sunk in God – then that very sense of an entire passivity which accompanies the soul's deepest action, of being, as Jacopone says, 'drowned in the Divine Sea', is surely one more tribute to the part played by symbolism in the normal process of the spiritual life.

And last, the essence of that life, *dedication of the will*. This of course is the ever-deepening temper of all personal religion worthy of the name. In its first movement it constitutes conversion; in its achieved perfection it is the very substance of the unitive life of the saint. But between those two points there is much work to be done and much suffering to be borne by those in whom this self-transcendence, this supernatural growth, is taking place. Because of the primary importance of God's overruling action, and yet also the great importance of the self's free and willing activity, there must be within any full spiritual life, at least until its final stages, a constant tension between effort and abandonment, loving communion and ethical struggle, illumination and purification, renunciation of the will and deliberate use of the will, as the natural and supernatural aspects of personality, both invaded and subdued to the divine purpose, come into play and the will of God for that soul is expressed in calls to concrete activity or to inward abandonment. So too in the actual life of prayer we ought to expect, and practise in some degree, both the deliberate effort of intercession and the abandoned quiet of contemplation. And as the soul grows in suppleness under these alternating stimulations – these 'stirrings and touches of God', as the mystics so realistically call them – so its sense of the divine action, which is always there but not always recognized, becomes more distinct and individuated until at last, in the full theopathetic life of the mystical saint, it becomes a perfectly responsive tool of the creative will. 'I live yet not I.' That of course is a real statement of experience, not a piece of piety; an experience which is reflected in the abnormal creative activities and spiritual power of the saints, from Paul of Tarsus to the Curé d'Ars.

And with this, I think, we reach the answer to the question with which we began: What exactly is the spiritual life? It is the life in which God and His eternal order have, more and more, their undivided sway; which is wholly turned to Him, devoted to Him, dependent on Him, and which at its term and commonly at the price of a long and costly struggle, makes the human creature a pure capacity for God. And as regards the actual prayer, the secret correspondence which accompanies this growth, this will tend mainly to fulfil itself along two paths: upwards to God in pure adoration – outward to the world in intercession. The interweaving of these two movements in the special way and degree in which they are developed by each soul, is the foundation of the spiritual life of humanity.

SOME IMPLICITS OF CHRISTIAN SOCIAL REFORM

✪

THERE IS AMONG CHRISTIAN MEN AND WOMEN A growing sense of the need of making the social order in which we live less inconsistent with the Spirit of Christ than it is at the present time: solving some of its most acute problems, and our own daily and hourly problems too, not in a spirit of compromise, but as Christian logic requires them to be solved. This is one of the most difficult of all tasks, for it means nothing less than the carrying through of the implicits of the spiritual world into every detail of the common life, bringing to bear on that recalcitrant common life the power and love given to us by our faith. And we must learn to look with humility, and also with intelligence – for this too is a gift of the Holy Ghost – at this supremely difficult thing, in order to learn how to set about it; for we have no doubt now that we must set about it, if our present confusions and miseries are to be healed. We cannot walk down a street of any of our larger towns without meeting the challenge of Christ.

Christian men and women. That means to us, of course, not what Jacob Boehme used to call 'mere historical new men' but living members of the mystical fellowship of the living Christ; members as it were of the great secret society of the universe, pledged to perfectly concrete and practical obligations, to the conscious furthering of the purposes of God. Conscious members too of that supernatural fellowship which St John declares to be the primary fact of the Christian life. 'Truly our fellowship is with the Father and with His Son . . . if we walk in the light, as He is in the light, we have fellowship one with another.' Fellowship here of course does not mean merely companionship, but utmost communion, oneness. Those who have experienced something of this reality and surrendered themselves, at least in will and intention, to all that it demands, can hardly regard themselves in any other light than as partners with Christ in the great and continual business of bringing the world of time into ever closer harmony with the eternal love and perfection of God.

The poet Donne said of Christ, in his sonnet on the Resurrection,

> He was all gold when He lay down, but rose
> All tincture . . .

He was using the language of the alchemists, whose final aim was to make, not merely gold, but a tincture that would transmute into gold all the baser metals that it touched. In this phrase he seems to have caught and expressed the Christian secret: that the living Christ is a tincture, not added to life but transmuting life wherever He enters it; and therefore that we must seek to bring under that influence not only the souls of individuals, but the corporate soul too, and so effect its transmutation. It is this change, not the imposition of a new moral code, which we should mean by the Christianization of society; for Christian law can only be understood and practised by Christian souls. Such a Christianization of society involves, ultimately, the complete interpenetration of God and human life; the drenching of life, on all its levels, with the divine charity – its complete irradiation by the spirit of goodness, beauty and love. This is fellowship with God, and nothing less than this ideal is fully Christian because nothing less than this fully works out the incarnational idea and gives all life its opportunity of reaching life's best levels in Christ. To say that this is impossible, is to say that spirit cannot triumph, and so to deny the very foundations of our faith.

We turn from thoughts of this kind and look round at the intricate and many-graded life of this planet, still holding tight to the conception of that life in its wholeness, as material for the working out of the incarnational idea: material of which the dominant character is that it can be so used – so entinctured by the divine reason, Christ – as to make of it a graded revelation of God. Look particularly at the bit of life for which we are plainly responsible: the order of so-called Christian civilized society. That, supremely, is the material for the working out of the incarnation to its full term. It was confided to us. Here we are, or can be, the actual tools through which the Divine Wisdom works out His purpose of perfection. Real Christianity, real consecration, means becoming such a tool.

There is a celebrated chapter in the *Visions and*

Revelations of that great mystic and spiritual teacher Angela of Foligno, which tells how, soon after her conversion, as she was walking alone through the vineyards between Spello and Assisi, she heard the Holy Spirit saying to her, wherever she looked, 'Behold and see! This is my creation.' And gazing on that exquisite landscape, bathed as it is in the light which we see in Perugino's pictures – a light which seems to be the veil of a more spiritual loveliness – she was filled with an ineffable sweetness and joy. And then all her sins and errors came back into her mind, and she was possessed by a humility such as she had never known before. We can translate that scene for ourselves, thinking of such a spring as that which we had this year: the beauty of the untouched English country, snowy with hawthorn, the downs starred with tiny perfect flowers, the amazing emerald life of the young beechwoods, the exultant singing of the birds – and the Spirit of God saying still in our hearts 'Behold and see! This is My creation!' We too, seeing this living and intricate beauty, were surely filled with gratitude and delight.

But now, reverse this picture; and suppose that we are condemned to go with Christ to some of the places which we, in our corporate capacity – Christian citizens of a Christian country – have made, or allowed through stupidity and sloth to come into existence. Imagine any one of us walking through the East End of London, or up the staircase of a lodging-house in Notting Dale – and then through Piccadilly, and up some staircases which one could find near there – or down our prison corridors – or through a poison-gas factory – with that companion at our side. And suppose that it is our turn to meet that glance and say 'Behold and see! This is our creation.' We can each complete that episode; but none without shame. Even to think of the contrast is surely to be possessed in our turn by such a penitence as we have never known before.

If we dare to complete the episode, to turn from this monumental exhibition of our corporate failure in intelligence and love, our greed, apathy, stupidity, lack of energetic faith, and look at the face of Christ – then we cannot feel any doubt about the nature of the command which is laid on us. We have to meet that vision fair and square – that infinite love and compassion which ought to be our love and compassion too – with the knowledge in our minds that there are places in all our great cities where it is not possible for a child to grow up in unsullied purity. This is our creation. We know what Jesus thinks about children and He brings to us the mind of God. Again, complete classes of the population are kept in a state of economic insecurity, which thwarts for them all chance of spiritual development; and we must hold such spiritual development – by which I do not mean piety – to be God's will for all people.

There is a level of deprivation and anxiety, just as there is a level of luxury, at which the soul's life cannot prosper; where animal interests and anxieties alone can survive. This poverty is not holy and simple, but sordid and degrading; and this is our creation too. It makes stunted, diseased, imperfect, wasted lives; ugliness, bitterness and tension. The soul's inherent beauty and possibility are taken and twisted out of shape by our worse than animal acquisitiveness, our steady self-occupation and indifference to the common good.

Christ demands the surrender of acquisitiveness, and ultimately a social order in which we can say to all men and women without irony, in respect of their bodily necessities, 'Your heavenly Father knoweth that ye have need of all these things: but seek ye first the kingdom of God and His righteousness and all these things shall be added unto you.' That alone – the corporate security which comes from the practical application of neighbourly love – is Christian citizenship. I do not say that this means the triumph of any particular *ism*; but it does mean, plainly, a triumph of the love and generosity of God in the heart and mind and strength of every individual of which that social order is built. Energy and intelligence, as well as mere feeling, dedicated to the purposes of Christ – and then brought to bear on the desperate problems of our corporate life. We have got that corporate life into such a mess now by our persistent acquiescence in a policy of clutch, that its problems seem to present insuperable difficulties; but there are no insuperable difficulties to divine love. It is strange that any Christian should look upon such a notion as fantastic, since it is merely the corollary of our faith in the power and present work of the Holy Spirit within life. Because of this faith we do not look upon it as fantastic; and we do look upon the social order which neglect of Christian realism has brought into being, as grotesque. Therefore we are bound to consider, in a spirit of prayer and with an entire willingness to pay the necessary price, how best to tackle some of the problems which have been brought into being by this triumph of acquisitiveness over love.

This involves a preliminary problem, to be faced by each of us: how to acquire, and hold, that attitude of mind and heart which will make us the most efficient tools of the Spirit of Christ and keep us in a measure – as He was supremely – at one and the same time hidden in God, yet wholly dedicated to His unstinted service, the furthering of His aim in our fellow-men. We shall only be useful in this work in so far as we achieve this, speaking and acting as men and women of prayer whose souls are opened wide towards the world of spirit and have received its penetrating gift of energy and peace. We must have the habit of recourse to eternity and its values must respond directly to God quite as often, and in as real, devoted, and intimate a spirit of love and service, as we respond to our fellow human beings. He is the one Reality, the one Touchstone, His revelation in Christ the pattern from which we must never depart, bringing to it every practical question and difficulty.

Professor Lethaby, in a recent book on town planning, appealed for the fostering in men and women – and specially in children – of the sense of the sacredness of their town: of its comeliness, dignity, beauty as the outward expressions of the corporate soul, something which all could love and seek to further and preserve. If we had this, we should come to feel that hideous buildings, vulgar advertisements and, still more, bad and degraded housing conditions were actual insults offered to the Spirit of God; and we should perhaps try instead to do honour to His holy power in our constructive work, considering all its problems in that Universal Spirit to which George Fox was always inviting us to have recourse. But this means a firm grasp of the fact of God's presence, a perpetual keeping of the pattern in focus; and this is not to be had unless we pay attention to it.

In the *Yearly Meeting Epistle* of the Society of Friends for 1920, the question was asked: How can we gain a new spirit? How can we break loose from our fears and suspicions and from the grip of complacent materialism, and face the issues with new faith in God and humanity? And the answer is: Only by a fresh sense of the presence and character of God. I am convinced that this is the right answer and the key to success in the work which we want to do. In the long run 'we behold that which we are', say the mystics, 'and are that which we behold'. Our outward lives inevitably come to harmonize with our real ideals; our vision of truth depends upon truth within. As our hearts are, so do our aim and our treasure come to be. This is true of society as well as of individual souls; the corporate life of a people that beholds the Eternal Beauty will tend to be beautiful in its turn. Psychology is insisting more and more on the importance of that which it calls the imagined end: the need of placing before our inner vision a clear picture of that which we want to achieve. This imagined end acts as a magnet, drawing and unifying our will, energy and desire. Whether our aim be health, success or holiness, the same principle applies: we tend towards that which we clearly envisage as possible and really desire. In this enterprise, then, it is above all things necessary that we should give ourselves a chance of looking at the end – the Kingdom, the realization of the love of God – and that we should constantly look, watch, listen, for the intimations of eternity and judge by this majestic standard the sins and omissions, the cheap expedients and selfish negligences, which enter into our dealings with the temporal environment within which our wills operate. Be still, and know, in order that you may be. Realize the superb possibilities of your material, the august power of creation that has been put into your hands; and do not conceive life in terms of jerry-built villas with garage attached. Look at your pattern, instead of working by rule of thumb. Seek spiritual food and give yourselves time to assimilate it, so that you may be strong. Before we can mend our unreal confusions, we must have a clear vision of the real; and the gaining and holding of such a vision in personal life is one of the main functions of prayer, as in corporate life its holding up is the chief business of institutional religion. Efforts to Christianize our social conduct are foredoomed unless those who undertake them give themselves time to look steadily at Christ.

Beyond this vision of the pattern, perpetually blurred, perpetually to be renewed if we would be true to it, there is also the question of power. Christianity is a religion of power; if it were not so, our undertaking would be hopeless. Recourse in prayer to the unchanging and eternal is recourse to the very sources of our life. The saying in the Fourth Gospel, 'I am come that they might have life, and have it more abundantly', is a practical, not merely a devotional, statement. *Zoe*, the 'more abundant life' offered to every real Christian, is not anything vague or metaphysical. It means, in modern jargon, a real enhancement of our life-force, that mysterious vital energy of which the Spirit of God is declared to be Lord and giver, and which conditions our body and mind, showing itself in our power of dealing with circumstances. This is an absolutely practical promise, making a sharp division between the person who only believes in Christianity, and the person who experiences it. Christian regeneration is not only a supernatural but also a psychological fact, which enhances efficiency, feeds power, gives life; and it does this by the sublimation of our vigorous instinctive nature, its unification and total dedication to one end. It really does initiate a series of changes in us – often slow and painful – which can bring us in the end, if we do not shirk them, into perfect and life-giving harmony with the will of God.

Therefore we bring to our study of the Christian social order and how we can work for it, this principle: that only by constantly looking at the pattern can we keep ourselves fine tuned for this job, and only by recourse to supernatural sources of power can we get the strength to put it through. History proves this to us. It shows us, again and again, that men and women of prayer tap a source of energy, possess a tranquil courage, an initiative, a faith, entirely unknown to those who have not set up and deliberately maintained through thick and thin these willed and loving contacts with the eternal life in which we 'live and move and have our being'. And it warns us most solemnly that, entering – as I believe we are entering – one of humanity's recurrent efforts to actualize the Spirit of Christ, we defeat our own purpose, cut ourselves off from the true fountain of that more abundant life which we shall need for it, unless we so order our existence that the life towards God keeps pace with the life lived for our fellow human beings.

There is in William Blake's 'Jerusalem' a marvellous drawing of the pitiful and energizing Spirit of Christ brooding over Albion, stretching His wounded hands to those two limits which Blake calls Adam and Satan – all the possibilities of our humanity (for Christ is, after all, the Son of man) and all the worst we have become. It seems to me we too are bound to strive for such a spiritual gesture, the stretching out as it were of one hand towards His perfection, the limit where divine and human meet, and of the other, in complete friendliness and generosity, towards the sins and imperfections of human beings. Neither action is particularly easy in a practical way, but unless we try to manage this, we need not regard ourselves as genuine friends of Christ. It is the double, simultaneous outstretching that matters; this only can open the heart wide enough to let in God and so make of each person who achieves it a mediator of His reality to other people. The non-religious socialist seems to stretch out one hand, and the non-social pietist the other. But one without the other is useless. Both at once: that is where the difficulty comes in. It sometimes seems a demand which we can hardly meet.

Mediators of God's reality to other people: this is to be in our small way workers with Christ. It means the constant interpretation to us of God's thought and will by the living Spirit, known to us in the life of prayer, and its constant handing on by ourselves in the active life of human intercourse and service. It means the translation of unchanging perfection – the pure reality of eternal life – into human terms: such concrete human terms as national, civic, industrial and family relationships. It means this actualization of God, given to us spiritually in all that we mean by the contemplative side of life, and laying on us the obligation of expressing it on the practical side of life. Never one without the other. Not the life of devotion divorced from the effort to bring in, here and now, the Kingdom of God; not, most certainly, the hopeless effort to actualize the Kingdom without the life of prayer. We want to bring the creative spirit of love – perpetually offered to us but never forced on us – to bear on the actual stuff of human life; and for this, we must make strong and close contacts with both orders, the spiritual and the human worlds.

St Teresa said that to give our Lord a perfect service, Martha and Mary must combine. The modern tendency is to turn from the attitude and the work of Mary and even call it – as I have heard it called by busy social Christians – a form of spiritual selfishness. Thousands of devoted men and women today believe that the really good part is to keep busy, and they give themselves no time to take what is offered to those who abide quietly with Christ because there seem such a lot of urgent jobs for Martha to do. The result of this can only be a maiming of their human nature, exhaustion, loss of depth and of vision; and it is seen in the vagueness and ineffectuality of a great deal of the work that is done for God. It means a total surrender to the busy click-click of the life of succession – nowhere, in the end, more deadly than in the religious sphere. I insist on this because I feel, more and more, the danger in which we stand of developing a lopsided Christianity so concentrated on service, and on this-world obligations, as to forget the need of constant willed and quiet contact with that other world, from whence the sanctions of service and the power in which to do it proceed. For those who are seeking to solve the problems of citizenship in a Christian light, that willed contact is of primary importance; so too is the inward discipline, the exacting, personal, secret effort and response, to which we shall find it impels us. Do you suppose that we can, so to speak, hop into our uniforms, let enthusiasm avail for efficiency, and win the battle thus? Most certainly not. We all believe now in education for citizenship, training for social service. Far more should we believe in training for spiritual service, for participation in the building of the City of God; and this has not much in common with what commonly passes for religious education. It means in practice the effort to live some sort of inner life harmonious with the great principles of Christian spirituality: penitence, renunciation, self-surrender, and daily recourse to the peace and power of God.

Here, then, those who desire to work most fruitfully for the Kingdom have a most delicate discrimination to make. Plainly it is not Christian to concentrate too much attention upon one's own soul; yet on the other hand, our own inward growth does condition both our communion with God and our power of helping other men. We see this double strain in all great religious teachers and in all the best helpers of humanity. It is exhibited on a grand scale in St Paul, St Augustine, St Francis, St Teresa, Fox, Wesley, in all of whom an unremitting, intense inner effort, an exacting life of self-discipline and prayer, an alert sensitiveness to the presence of God, kept pace with outward deeds. Remember Elizabeth Fry, balancing her marvellous regenerative work by silent worship. Remember General Booth travailing in spirit and creating the Salvation Army. The breezy modern doctrine which we so often hear recommended – go straight ahead, fill your life to the brim with service, and your soul will take care of itself – this notion receives no support whatever from the real heroes of practical Christianity. They were keenly aware of their own disharmonies and inward conflicts, and felt these to be a source of weakness, as they are. They knew they must resolve these conflicts, if the Holy Spirit was to work through them without impediment, if they were to grow and achieve the stature in which they could best do the work of Christ. So in them, penitence kept pace with love, and prayer with work. Conscious loving dependence on greater sources of power – fellowship with God – was the cause of their success; and the fact that our Lord's own teaching and works of power and mercy appear closely dependent on the nights which He spent on the mountain in prayer, might make us hesitate about abandoning this, the classic norm of Christian life. The effort towards Christian citizenship, in fact, must begin by the effort to be, ourselves, each one of us, citizens of the City of God.

The English mystic, Walter Hilton, has a beautiful and celebrated passage in which he describes pilgrim man travelling in desire towards that city: how he sees it on a hill, small and far away, yet real, as a pilgrim first sees Jerusalem. It seems to him at that distance very tiny, hardly more than a rood in length; nevertheless he knows it to be no mere vision, but the true home of his soul. When he reaches it, he finds it is within 'both long and large, that without was so little to his sight', a very roomy place, full of every kind of dwelling, a home for all manner of people: and he discovers that this city he has been journeying towards so long is nothing else but that concrete love of God to which the soul attains when it ascends the Mount of Contemplation. And Hilton ends his parable thus:

> This city betokeneth the perfect love of God, set in the hill of contemplation; the which, to the sight of a soul that without the feeling of it travelleth towards it in desire, seemeth somewhat, but it seemeth but a little thing, no more than a rood, that is six cubits and a palm of length. By six cubits are understood the perfection of a man's work; and by the palm, a little touch of contemplation . . . nevertheless, if he may come within the city of contemplation, then seeth he much more than he saw first.

Consider this well; for here we have a formula by which to fine tune our own conceptions of citizenship in the Kingdom of God. It demands two things: 'the perfection of a man's work, and a little touch of contemplation'. That means the union of skill and vision, both consecrated. One without the other is no good; we shall not get the measurement of the city right. Accept then this conception of the Kingdom of God on earth, as built up by humanity's very best work, directed by humanity's very best prayer, and see what it must mean in efficiency and beauty, industry and joy. Take that measurement into slums, factories, schools, committee rooms, labour exchanges and building-estates – the perfection of a man's work and a little touch of contemplation – and then, measure against this scale ourselves and our average performances. The first result will probably be profound humiliation. We shall perceive ourselves, face to face with the social muddle, incapable of that perfection of work which its rebuilding requires and of the sharp vision of the pattern on the hill, which will give us faith in the possibility of actualizing it on earth in a Christian order of society. It is a long way off, hardly in focus yet; nevertheless, let us at least travel towards it, as Hilton asks us, in thought and desire.

With this thought in our minds, of the perfect union of work and of prayer demanded of us by Christ, if His purpose is to be fulfilled by His friends, look at the programme for this week. It points out to us three great forms of social wrongness, which inhibit the free action of God's will for human beings: our acquiescence first in materialism, next in the principle of conflict, and last in social and racial injustice. Where the love of God declared in Christ alone should rule, if we mean anything by Christianity, these three things rule instead. If we look more closely, we see what they represent. Not so much humanity's wilful wrongness – though each offers opportunity and encouragement to all the lowest and most unloving impulses of human beings – but rather a failure to push forward, a relapse into those lower levels of life from which God, as we believe, is drawing out the human soul into His own light. They represent the natural tendency of human beings to camp in the marshes instead of undertaking the climb upwards to Jerusalem: their failure, as psychology would say, to sublimate and adapt to new levels the crude forms of that instinct of self-preservation which once under other conditions served them well. They show that our impulsive minds, which really control our actions, are still the impulsive minds of primitive people, ruled by fear and anger, pride and possessiveness, unredeemed by the Perfect Man revealed in Jesus.

Our materialism is the survival and accentuation of the necessary preoccupation of primitive peoples with the material world; the immense importance for them — if they were to survive at all — of food, shelter, possessions; the sense that they are valuable for their own sakes and, being won with difficulty, must be clutched tight as the very substance of their life. Our spirit of conflict, whether shown in industrial competition or international struggles, represents the survival of that pugnative instinct which impelled primitive people, in a world full of inimical forces, to fight for their own hand, their own family, their own tribe. Our class and racial antagonisms represent the wrong development of that herd-instinct which was perhaps one of the very first instruments of human social education; teaching people their first lessons in brotherhood, obedience, self-subordination to the common good, but also tending to assemble them in exclusive groups that are smaller than their capacity for love.

These antique tendencies, immensely strong, are now so cunningly disguised and rationalized that very few of us realize the half-savage and half-childish nature of the impelling instinct which causes us to love a bargain, to collect things for collecting's sake, to judge rich and poor by different standards, to resent a trespass, blindly to support our own class or country, to enjoy combative games and destructive sports, to feel uplifted by a patriotic song. None of these impelling instincts are wrong in themselves; but they are now occasions of wrong, because we have failed to sublimate them. We let them go on, in altered conditions, giving us suggestions appropriate to the Stone Age, instead of harnessing these vigorous springs of psychic energy to the chariot of Christ. To do this, (1) we must replace material by spiritual values – the respect for wealth by the respect for beauty, the desire for goods by the desire for good, the desire for luxury by the desire for justice; quantity by quality; must dissolve acquisitiveness in that spirit of poverty which enjoys everything because it desires nothing. (2) We must replace the belief in achievement through conflict and the defeat of our adversary – whether in the international, the economic or the political field – by belief in achievement through love, united effort, and the winning of our adversary: 'Loving the unlovely into loveableness.' (3) We must replace tyranny between class and race by love between class and race; fraternity, the true fulfilment of the herd instinct, overflowing its first narrow boundaries till it embraces the world.

But these are mental and spiritual imperatives; they spring up from within, they are not imposed from without. They remind us again that the Christian order of society can only come into being as the expression of a corporate Christian soul. If we want to produce it, we must first produce a corporate change of heart, bit by bit Christianizing the social body from within, so that it may become more and more incapable of acts that conflict with the principle of love, and of tolerating for others conditions which we would never allow to affect those individuals for whom we really care. Corporate regeneration must follow the same course as personal regeneration. Accepting, like the individual Christian, the incarnation as the clue to life, the community must grow into conformity with this belief. It can only do this along the same lines as the individual: namely, by a balanced process of analysis and synthesis. It must first track down and realize the true springs of its conduct, press back into the racial past and discover the humiliating facts about those impulses which really condition our behaviour in such matters as nationalism, property, employment, servitude, sex. It must acknowledge how many notions necessary to a primitive state of society have become imbedded in our view of life and, thanks to the conservative nature of the social mind, still govern our corporate view of existence. It must further realize that these relics of the past, however imposing the disguises they now wear in financial and political circles, represent something less than humanity's best here and now possibility; and that therefore our wholesale capitulation to them, our quiet assumption that you cannot go against 'human nature' in its most acquisitive, self-regarding and combative mood, has the character of sin.

Having reached this level of self-knowledge, the community may perhaps be brought to something equivalent to social penitence. It may feel as a direct reproach every life damaged by bad housing, every child maimed by economic conditions, every soul stifled by luxury or obsessed by unreal values, every man or woman embittered and made hopeless by unemployment and friendlessness. And then, turning in one way or another to God, to Reality, to the true values declared in Christ, the work of whose creative Spirit its mingled stupidity and selfishness retards, society may set in hand the complementary movement of synthesis: the real building-up of Jerusalem, by perfect work and steady prayer.

Let us take, as a last thought, a picture from current philosophy: that great vision of the so-called new realists, of a universe which has, as they say, a *tendency to deity* and is moving perpetually towards the actualization of God. That picture, for Christians, indeed for all truly religious minds, must be incomplete. Yet does it not represent, as far as it goes, a real view of the Holy Spirit dwelling within our world of change and ever seeking more perfect incarnation in life? And is it not humanity's supreme vocation to co-operate in this, consciously to forward the creative aim of divine love and share in the business of the spiritual world, which is lifting all things up into the order of Divine Reality? These may seem very metaphysical, possibly even unreal, considerations to put side by side with our pressing problems of internationalism, economics, family life. But philosophy reminds us again that unless we can set the particular details of our actual life within some such universal background, we shall never understand their significance; and that a first duty of thought is to get this universal background right. At present the universals within which we see our particular social order are wrong, because not Christian; hence the wrong interpretation is put upon particular facts and a wrong scale of values obtains. Our need, then, is the rebirth of our vast potential energies into a world of fresh values, in which each particular action would be given the meaning that it has for the mind of Christ. It is an exacting standard but we dare not aim at less, for we cannot forget that for Christians human nature, human love, and human life find their controlling law and their perfect fulfilment on Calvary, and not on any lower level than that. But to remember this, to keep our eye fixed on it, means living in the spirit of prayer; and to live up to it means an unremitting effort, both social and individual, to Christianize our every action through and through, and so fulfil the destiny of our souls.

THE CHRISTIAN BASIS
OF SOCIAL ACTION

✦

THERE IS A STRANGE LITTLE STORY IN THE EARLY ANNALS of the Franciscan Order of how Brother Giles, one of the holiest of the first companions of Francis, deeply shocked some Dominican friars by the casual observation that St John the Divine really says nothing at all about God. In answer to their horrified exclamations at this apparently profane utterance, Brother Giles went on to say that one might think of God as a mountain of grain, as great as the Monte Cetano which was towering above them, and of St John as no more than a sparrow, who picked here and there a few odd grains from that unmeasured richness, without making any real impression upon it at all. In which it appears to me that St John proved himself to be indeed the patron saint of all theologians.

It was with this searching little story in my mind that I read the terms of reference which are put before this Summer School, namely: 'To discover and to define the Catholic doctrinal basis for the Christian life, personal and social.' We are further told that we are successively to study from this point of view the world-order, the nation, the industrial order, and the home; and in the course of our explorations will have to consider three things:

(a) The implications of the Catholic faith in practical life.

(b) The distinctive Catholic principles on which social action should be based.

(c) The view that the manifold activities of life when rightly understood all come within the range of religion and constitute a unity in God that theology must express.

Considering these statements over against the mysterious presence of God, I then began to wonder which among the particular grains of truth that humanity has brought home from the mountain were to be regarded as 'specific Catholic doctrines' It sometimes seems to me that the distinction between Catholic and non-Catholic is not a very fruitful one, and that the distinction between those who do, and those who do not, love and adore God revealed in Christ and refer all things to Him, goes deeper into the reality of things. But if we keep to the language of our syllabus, and try to define the essence of Catholic Christianity, I suppose the first things that come to mind are the Catholic emphasis on the incarnation and its continuance in the sacraments, and the concept of the absolute value and authority of the Church as the Mystical Body of Christ.

When, however, we look further, these doctrines are seen to derive their deepest significance from the fact that they are special demonstrations and developments of one overruling truth; which we might call the priority of the supernatural and its presence and revelation in and through the natural. Catholicism requires the central truth of God as Spirit and Father of Spirits, the one Absolute Reality; and of this God-Spirit, as eternal, loving, personal, prevenient and self-revealed – supremely in what we call the incarnation, continuously in various degrees in the sacraments of religion and of life. If we accept this philosophic position, our first proposition will then be that Catholic doctrine is uncompromisingly theocentric. For it, in the last resort, only God matters. And this at once means that the Catholic can never consent to *mere* social and material betterment, as being in itself a sufficient Christian ideal. We are called to seek perfection – all kinds of perfection – only because God is perfect first. So if we wish to discuss our first term of reference – the Catholic doctrinal basis of the Christian life – we must look first at the Catholic idea of God and the soul's relation to Him. Of course the real virtue and the doctrinal heart of any religion is always decided by its idea of God; and Christian effort in the past has often failed through forgetfulness of this. And it is that richly living concept of God's concrete reality and utter distinctness from the world, yet His ceaseless activity within and for every bit of it, escaping monism on the one hand and deism on the other, which is decisive for Catholicism. We must balance that deep, awed sense of the transcendent mystery of the mountain which alone is truly religious, by the certitude that even the sparrow can and must go there for its food.

This position means that the Catholic attitude towards existence can never be merely naturalistic or this-world. It can never permit religion to become merely an aid to the full and virtuous living out of the natural life. It fixes the mind, not on the possible perfecting of the animal creation, but on the ever-growing and never-finished perfecting of the spiritual creation. It must refuse to attribute absolute value to the world of change, save in so far as it incarnates the Unchanging. It requires a constant sense of mystery, depth, the supernatural; it is, in fact, a two-step religion.

Again, Catholic philosophy can never regard as complete any theory of the spiritual life based on self-development from within; nor can it consent to the doctrine of the soul as an impenetrable monad, or expound the possibilities, apprehensions and experiences of that soul on the basis of 'unpacking its own portmanteau, and explaining itself to itself'. Everywhere in life, though in varying degrees, it requires and finds the prevenient presence and action of something other than nature: the vivid reality of grace, Spirit, God. Thus it rests on a profound duality, which goes right through religious experience and must govern our view of personal and social life: the distinctness and over-againstness of the eternal and the historical, of God and the soul, of grace and nature.

Yet, on the other hand, Catholicism emphatically declares an intimate contact between all these pairs of opposites. Spiritual reality is not and never can be cut off from the world of sense. There is at every point a penetration of the world by God, a truth which of course underlies the doctrine of the Holy Spirit. Hence the God of supernature is also the God of nature; and it is not Christian to say that the *world* is very evil, although *we* often are. Christianity says that the Father of the eternal wisdom is the father of the sparrow too.

This emphasis on the overruling reality and distinctness of the supernatural, yet refusal to make watertight compartments between it and the natural, covers, I think, all the affirmations most distinctive of Catholicism: the incarnation considered both as a general truth and as historical fact, sacramentalism, the communion of saints. It commits the Catholic at least to a modified dualism. It commits us to the view that the spiritual life of humanity is not completely articulated unless it has an inside and an outside too: and that in so far as we are aware of spiritual values, we are bound to try to give them adequate expression in the world of sense. It rejects mere unbridled immanence on the one hand, and a sharp separation between God and the sense-world on the other hand. It recognizes that matter and sense do play their part in all contacts between God and the soul, and that therefore the phenomenal world has and retains true importance even in the loftiest reaches of spirituality. And here it provides a point of departure for discovering the method and aim of Christian social action. Such a view is consistent with the general trend of the great New Testament writers. Indeed, the first clause of the Lord's Prayer at once commits us to the view that we are creatures of supernatural affinities, that our real status cannot be understood merely as a development from within the natural order, for this only tells half the truth about the soul. And the whole of the spiritual life can be regarded as a progressive realization of this truth, as we expand into fuller personal being: deeper, humbler and more loving awareness of God. From one point of view all real human progress means such spiritualization – in technical language, a growth in and a yielding to grace – and the practices of religion are the food and helps of this growth.

If then we regard human life, corporate and individual, from this angle, where shall we stop? Where are the frontiers of human life and possibility to be fixed? And how shall we reconcile such a thoroughgoing other-worldliness with our obvious this-world obligations? This is a problem which ought to be before the minds of all social reformers. As Catholic Christians they cannot logically acquiesce in any schemes for the making of a social order, however otherwise desirable, that will oppose or check in any way the trend and expansion of the soul's supernatural energy. They can never accept the Utopia of the kind-hearted materialist or give comfort, safety, even political freedom, the rank of a Christian ideal. Civilization and spiritualization are not the same thing; and for the Christian, spiritualization must always come first. On the other hand, we are bound to work for the elimination, here and now, of all conditions hostile to that spiritualization, all checks on the soul's healthy life. Thus the many things which are plainly hostile – drink, prostitution, bad housing, tyranny, reduced moral standards, embittered class or race relationships – become of intense importance, even, and perhaps specially, to the most thoroughgoing supernaturalist; and are all matters with which religion ought to deal.

But we cannot stop there. Such a general view of the intimate relation of the natural and spiritual is not sufficient unless it is regarded as the preparation and incentive for action. The recognition that God acts within life by means of the material order brings with it, or should bring, a further recognition that we in our turn are called upon to be the creative instruments of God in space and time, co-operating according to our measure in the ceaseless loving action of His Spirit upon life. The sparrow in whose beak a grain of the living manna has been placed is therefore bound in its strength to do its best for the sparrow world. True, religion will deal best with the problem of evil by its own method of individual inward sanctification, which was the method of Christ. But such personal sanctification is the first of two movements. It is only in the exceptional and purely contemplative nature that the obligation to incarnate God's will, further the redemptive action of the Holy Spirit, can be met by devotional self-expression alone; and even in such natures, the more purely the flame of contemplation burns, the more in the end it is found to inspire saving action. This proposition could be illustrated again and again from the lives of the saints. We cannot sit down and be devotional while acquiescing in conditions which make it impossible for other souls even to obey the moral law. For it is not God who imposes such an impossibility. It is we, in the corporate sense, who do so; and we have no right to ask God to mend conditions unless we are willing to be ourselves the tools with which the work is done.

The obligation to do something about this seems to me to rest with crushing weight on every Christian communicant, for reasons which are too sacred to be given detailed discussion here. But at least we can say that there must be a sense in which the whole world and everything in it is sacred to us because God loves it; and therefore we are committed to doing our best in, with and for it – our best physically and mentally, as well as our best spiritually. I should like to see the Ignatian act of consecration recited after all those prayers in which we ask the divine love to do something about the social and industrial miseries our Christian civilization has produced: 'Take, Lord, and receive all *my* liberty; *my* memory, *my* understanding, *my* will, all I have and possess.'

There are, I suppose, two main ways of taking religion. The religious soul may withdraw more and more from the world and the life of the senses, in order to go by the path of negation to God. Or it may merge itself by love and surrender in the creative will of God and, in and with that will, go out towards the whole world. This, of course, is the way of Christianity. Thus we arrive by another path at the conclusion already stated: that the God of the natural and of the supernatural is one, and therefore, though physical and spiritual must ever be distinguished, they must never be put into opposite camps, for this rends the Body of Christ. The rushing out of Christ's love and admiration towards flowers, birds, children, all the simple joyous unspoilt creations of God, was part of the same movement, the same passionate desire to further the glory of God in His creatures, which showed itself in acts of healing, compassion, and forgiveness towards disease and sin, and in anger and indignation towards selfishness, meanness and hypocrisy. All these were various exhibitions of the perfect harmony of His soul with the Spirit that loves and upholds the world.

Thus adoration can never exempt the Christian from this-world action; and this-world action, however beneficial, will fail of effect if its foundations are not based upon the life of adoration. To go back to Brother Giles's parable, the sparrow must go to the mountain; but it must also live the common sparrow life, build its nest and feed its young. The awed sense of the mystery in which we live, and which enfolds and penetrates us, must not stultify our small human activities, but improve them. It is by this alternation of the transcendent and the homely, the interaction of lofty thought and concrete thing – all the friction and effort consequent on our two-levelled human life – that the true growth of human personality is achieved.

We put all this in more philosophic language when we say that being a Christian, loving God, 'finding and feeling the Infinite', does not absolve us from being part of history or from a full entrance into, and dealing with, the life of succession. On the contrary, it commits us to the task of trying to work out God's purpose in history. Even the contemplative vocation is entirely misunderstood by us if we suppose its essence to consist in a solitary and purely spiritual relationship to God. It is, in its fullest expansion, a special arduous and sacrificial method of dealing with the sins and discords of life. The duty towards which any incarnational philosophy points us is the bringing forth within historical succession of more and more of that abiding power, the 'something insusceptible of change', which transcends history. The true life and wonder of the human soul consists in its power of embracing and combining both these terms: the fact that it is able to be intimately concerned both with being and with becoming. And the same is, or should be, true of the corporate soul of society.

Now since what philosophy calls the 'absolute values' are statements about the character of God, though of course incomplete statements – grains picked by the sparrow off the mountain – it is plainly a part of this ability and duty of the soul to try to incarnate these absolute values within that order, that world of succession, with which we are able to deal. The Parable of the Talents hints that the common practice of giving them decent burial in consecrated ground, instead of taking the risks involved in putting them out to interest, is not in accordance with the vigour and realism of the mind of Christ. St Augustine's 'My life shall be a real life, being wholly full of Thee' sums up, from this point of view, the Catholic standard both of individual and social action. We must desire this deeper realness not for ourselves only, but for all people, and for all those institutions in which people are combined – since we are called to love all other souls as much as our own, and God above all souls – and must oppose and try to eliminate all that conflicts with such expansion of personality. The doctrinal basis for Christian action then becomes the obligation to make the world of life such that it can be wholly full of God, that His Kingdom may come and His will be done unimpeded by anything which we can rectify, as fully within the historical order as in the eternal scene. For the real theme alike of Catholic philosophy and Catholic sacramentalism is the continuing intimate presence of God in history and His revelation through historical processes, historical persons, sensuous symbols and impressions. The bold Athanasian epigram 'He became human that we might become divine' at least warns us against any inhuman aloofness from the natural world. That natural world, that historical order can never of course be adequate to Him but are nevertheless destined, according to their measure, to incarnate His life and convey it. Anything which contributes to this end has a right to our support and sympathy. Anything which blocks the way to it we must regard as an evil, and as the proper object of Christian attack.

Thus, in refusing to do our best to improve and purify the social order, we are refusing the religious obligation to make it, in so far as we can, a fit vehicle of the Spirit of God. Redemption is bound to have its this-world aspect; and it is perhaps its this-world aspect which is specially committed to our care. Hurried transcendentalists do well to ponder the extent to which our Lord's short ministry was concerned with the homely details of human life. 'I have felt', said John Woolman the Quaker, 'a longing in my mind that people might come into cleanness of spirit, cleanness of person, cleanness about their houses and gardens; and I think even the minds of people are in some degree hindered from the pure operation of the Holy Spirit, where they breathe much of the bad air of towns.'

Here Woolman is surely in line with the homely and human spirituality of the New Testament, and its perpetual acknowledgement of the close interdependence of body and soul, of inward and outward things. Indeed, if the Creator be also the Father, and creates and redeems by and through a physical order, that physical order, once we really understand it, must turn out to be a thing of infinite importance and possibility. And the way to understand it is to love it. 'God so loved the world' involves a totally different theology from 'God so loved the souls in the world'. If, with Baron von Hügel, we agree that the human spirit is called to 'a humble creaturely imitation of the eternal spaceless Creator, under the deliberately accepted conditions, and doubly refracting media, of time and space', then this must involve in our own small way something of His loving, all-merciful, generous dealing with all the needs and problems of the world.

The first article of the Creed – I believe in God, Father Almighty, maker of heaven and earth – really contains within itself the full Christian obligation to deal with social problems. If the eternal Creator be indeed a Father caring even for the sparrows, this lays on us the duty of loving interest in all He cares for and sustains. The wider the circle of this love and interest of ours, the nearer it comes to embracing all created life – the more perfect, in other words, our charity – the nearer we are to the ideal set before human beings in Christ. The reality of the ascent of our spirits in communion and prayer can best be tested by the extent in which they 'flow out in love to all in common'. The intensity, and special field of action, of this outflowing interest will vary in individuals. But it is a function of the Body of Christ in which all are concerned.

If we accept these principles, then the real problem before us falls into two parts. First, what we ought to do, and why; secondly, what our ultimate objective ought to be.

What we ought to do, and why. We ought always to work for the elimination of any conditions which we could not tolerate for persons whom we love and which, on a higher plane, we see to be inconsistent with our best ideas of God. The reason why we ought to do this is because, for Catholic Christians, the sacramental principle is operative over the whole range of life, in countless ways and degrees, and they are obliged to hold that God comes to human beings through and in natural means. We must therefore improve those natural means in every department of experience. And we are bound to be personally active in this matter because our own sanctification is only the first of two movements, and is chiefly important as making us instruments with which the Spirit of God, indwelling history, does His work.

What our objective ought to be. The objective of the Christian supernaturalist must surely be a material world which will further in every possible way, for all people and at all levels, the life of the soul; a natural order which will be the matter of a sacrament expressing the supernatural. This does not mean the necessary elimination of pain, tension, difficulty, hard work, or temptation. It means seeking to make these, for all people, more and more contributory to the growth of spiritual personality, instead of hostile to it. Such a programme has nothing whatever in common with an ideal of general comfortableness. Christian conduct can never be actuated merely by humanitarian considerations. On the contrary, it seems to me that the Catholic sociologist must at least try to achieve a balance between the ascetic and the benevolent outlook and action, the balance which we see so perfectly achieved in Christ. Ascetic as regards the spiritual growth and purification of human beings; benevolent as regards their natural status and rights. Christian social reform is not merely the effort of a number of clever, kindhearted, well-intentioned animals to make things as pleasant and wholesome all round as they possibly can. So far as it is a genuine activity of the spirit, it is the response of our individual spirits to the pressure of God's creative love, our effort to let that love find ever fuller expression through our action – one of the ways in which the eternal Wisdom uses human personality 'as a man uses his own hand'. We do not bring to it a true sense of vocation until we feel this, and feel, too, that all in it which truly matters points beyond this world.

What do those searching and terrific sayings of Christ – perhaps the most terrific of all His utterances, when we realize their full implications – about the giving of a cup of cold water, the meat given or refused to the hungry, the receiving of the little child, really mean? What in fact is involved for us in the one saying which He makes decisive for the ultimate destiny of the soul?

> Inasmuch as ye have done it unto the least
> of these My brethren, ye have done it unto
> Me.

Surely there is something here far deeper and more drastic than a general invitation to 'good works' or the sentimentalisms of a certain type of pious philanthropy? Does not this bring us once more, from another point of departure, to a practical acknowledgement of the universal, intimate presence of the divine life in history, an extension of the incarnation which does not stop short of our humblest experiences, and which means that our attitudes and acts towards our fellows are always in this sense attitudes and acts towards God? This discovery of the eternal God in other people – in every grade and aspect of natural life – does not mean pantheism. But surely it does mean loving and doing all we can for these His lowly dwelling-places and manifestations among us, purifying and unselfing all human relationships. It means too that we cannot dare to claim the benefits of His self-identification with our interests, unless we in our turn are ready to identify ourselves with the interests of other people; not merely those interests we choose to call moral and religious, but every difficulty, longing and need. When Angela of Foligno, at her supreme moment of apprehension, exclaimed, 'The whole world is *full* of God!', did not this vision embrace a whole multitude of paths, those we call physical as well as those we call spiritual, along which God flows in on human beings, and may and will be reached and served by us so long as we truly mean and intend Him?

Such a view involves the possible consecration of every material act. Placed within this living and personal conception of the divine immanence, 'Inasmuch as ye have done it . . .' takes on fresh depth and almost unbearable poignancy. It means the discovery, within social contacts of every kind, of an opportunity for the direct service of eternal love – and this must involve far more than a mere unorganized kindliness. It means approaching the problems of social life with our heads as well as our hearts; remembering that it is within our power to make social science a department of theology. The apocryphal saying of Christ, 'Blessed art thou O Man if thou *knowest* that which thou dost do!', is supremely true of those who achieve this and marks the difference between the Christian social action which begins at the altar and comes back to the altar, and the merely ethical sort.

Now what have we said? Really this: that the ultimate doctrinal basis of Christian personal life and social action is that rich conception of God, as both transcendent to and immanent in His world, which it is the very business of Catholic worship to express in its intensest form. And further, that this conception of God, when it becomes to us a living, all-penetrating reality and not a theological statement, is found to require from us a life which spends itself in love and service on this world, whilst ever in its best expressions and aspirations pointing beyond it. A life, in fact, moving towards a goal where work and prayer become one thing, since in both the human instrument is completely surrendered to the creative purposes of God and seeks more and more to incarnate the Eternal. Since what is true of us one by one must surely as we rise into a fuller humanity become true of us in groups, we have here a principle which might at last become operative in our international, political and civic relationships. As corporate Christians we cannot be satisfied with a merely individual application of our faith. We must set as our goal such an expansion – through, in and with us – of creative and redeeming love as shall embrace the whole world and be operative on every level of our many-graded life.

What would the acceptance of such principles mean? It would mean that every Christian must work for a social order in which the outward would become ever more and more the true sacramental expression of the inward. And as an essential preliminary to this, much faithful purification of that outward; the disharmonies, atavisms, sterile passions and disguised self-seekings which the individual Christian is obliged to face and conquer on his way towards union with God, must also be identified and conquered by the group. Penitence has its social aspect; there, too, humanity is surely called upon to recognize a wrongness that can become a rightness, and the need of action as an earnest of contrition.

But the social order which should emerge from such a realistic correspondence with Reality would not be distinguished by a tiresome uniformity, or any oppressive and puritanical goodiness. It would possess a rich and inexhaustible variety in unity, for it is called to reflect a facet of the mind of that God Who loves children as well as students, and has created tomtits as well as saints. It would be a social order in which energy would not be wasted in mere conflict, in which every talent and vocation had its chance. It would give a great place to the contribution which those who seek truth and beauty make to our knowledge of God. It would recognize this world as a theatre of the Spirit. Whilst acknowledging and encouraging all innocent and legitimate fields of action, it would yet leave room for, and point to, a life beyond the world, giving fullest opportunity for the growth of those spiritual personalities in whom eternal values are incarnated and through and by whom holiness is glimpsed by us. A world-order in fact obedient to the God of supernature and of nature and permitting the fullest development, interplay and mutual support of the active and contemplative lives. For this and only this perpetuates within history the full and balanced Christian ideal. Only this permits human beings to incarnate according to their measure – and even under the simplest, most homely accidents – the eternal in human life. Thus they feed upon and make their own those few small grains they bring back from the mountain, whilst yet recognizing and adoring, beyond the possible span of all these, their little discoveries and realizations, the unmeasured and unsearchable richness of God.

THE IDEALS OF THE
MINISTRY OF WOMEN

❂

WE SHALL ALL FEEL IT UNDESIRABLE THAT THE LAST
speaker at such a conference as this should
introduce any controversial note. But I feel bound in
honesty to state in a few words my own position in
regard to the main issue, before I go on. I am opposed to
the giving of the priesthood to women for many
reasons, and chiefly because I feel that so complete a
break with Catholic tradition cannot be made save by
the consent of a united Christendom. Any local or
national Church which makes it will drop at once to the
level of an eccentric sect. On the other hand, I greatly
desire and also expect an immense extension and
recognition of women's ministry in other directions than
this. Properly 'rooted and grounded' in lives of real
simplicity and self-abandonment, this must conduce to
the well-being and enriching of the Church's life. Hence
the great importance for the future of a right conception
of our situation: what we have to give, and how we can
best give it. But these, after all, are merely the views of
one insignificant individual looking out on the external
situation, and any individual view of that external

situation, how it should and how it may develop, is mostly guesswork at the best. We do not want to end there, but rather to remind ourselves once more of those realities on which anything pleasing to God in our work must depend. If we are true to those realities and seek to increase our hold upon them, then surely, whatever our status as workers for the Church and whatever recognition we may or may not get, we shall be able to be useful to Him and to souls. And that, and that alone, is the point.

What, after all, *is* Christian ministry, male or female, lay or ecclesiastical? It is, or should be, just the attempt of someone who cares supremely about God to cherish and help in one way or another the souls that are loved by God: to be as one that serveth. And moreover it is an attempt that is made, not because we feel like it or choose it, but because we are decisively pressed, called, put to it. 'You have not chosen me, but I have chosen you.' The word vocation does not mean that we do the calling. It is true, alas, that we often seem to see this principle ignored; but is it worthwhile to consider the sort and degree of pastoral work which we *might* do, unless we are prepared to do everything which comes our way from that centre? 'Lovest thou me? Feed my sheep.' That is the real point, isn't it? and the only one. Over against that, all discussions about our call and status, and what we ought to be allowed to do, and what we have to contribute, and whether the shepherds accept us as trained shepherdesses, or more often regard us as auxiliary dogs – all that fades into silence.

That real teaching saint, Father Benson of Cowley, said: 'It is a sign of perfection to be willing to do anything', yes, even under the orders of the curate you don't much like. Supple, equal to any burden and any job, because the burden of one's own importance has been given up. Surely a body of women aiming at that type of perfection would do more for God than a body of women who had achieved some particular status. The work that endures, and that is worthwhile, comes always from an immense self-surrender; and only that kind of ministry is going to increase the power and vitality of the Church. It really is not worth our while to struggle for the opportunity of giving anything less than that. No kind of assertiveness whatsoever can serve the purpose of the supernatural life. That merely blocks the divine right of way, prevents the Spirit from getting through. If it is true — and I think perhaps it is true — that the movement of that Spirit within the Church is opening fresh paths along which women can serve God and souls; then how careful we must all be to balance our initiative and devotedness by great patience, suppleness, and self-oblivion. We surely cannot wish to give up the sacred privilege of the lowest place.

Here we must try to avoid doctrinaire conclusions which arise from disguised self-will, and be entirely at the disposal of God. Do you remember the beautiful story of the Vision of Pier Pettignano? He saw the Church Visible as a superb procession following after Christ on the Way of the Cross, all the ecclesiastics, dignitaries, and officials each in their place and each with their credentials. And at the end of it all came the shabby little figure of St Francis, in his patched tunic, with no credentials, no position, drawn only by love. And he alone was walking in the very footsteps of the

Crucified.

I have known a few women in my life who have genuinely ministered to souls in a creative way, who truly gave the living water and the heavenly food. They have all been extremely simple and unpretentious. The question of status, scope and so forth has never, I should think, entered their minds at all. Their hidden life of love and prayer – and here surely is a capital point – has largely exceeded and entirely supported their life of active work. That, it seems to me, is the ministry which the Church so desperately wants; and if we are ever to give it, it means that our inner life towards God must be twice – no, ten, a hundred times – more vivid, constant and courageous than anything our active life may demand of us. For only thus can we ever begin to learn charity; and it is only in charity that men and women can minister to each other spiritual things. How else indeed could turbulent, half-made, self-willed creatures like ourselves hope to keep themselves at the disposal of God? If He is to find in us fresh channels of His life-giving life, the proportion of our hidden prayer to our active life must be the proportion of root to tree. But are we prepared, do you think, for all that such a scheme of life will cost us, the tremendous training it will mean, and the reversal of values it involves? A return, in fact, to the values of the New Testament. And if not, is it worth while to worry about our external scope?

Movements and demands, however legitimate, can be actually dangerous if they deflect attention from the one thing that is needful to the many things that may be useful or expedient. So, if there *is* to be a new movement in the Church, a removal of barriers and a new opportunity of pastoral service for women, how terribly careful we should be that it begins in a movement of the heart, and that this movement should be, as von Hügel says, vertical first and horizontal afterwards. Don't you think that what the Church needs most is not more and more officials but more and more people freely self-given for love? People who work from the centre, and radiate God because they possess Him; people in whom, as St Teresa said, Martha and Mary combine. No use getting Martha that splendid up-to-date gas cooker if you have to shove Mary out of the way to find a place where it can stand.

Just notice those women in the past who have ministered with most conspicuous success to souls, the heads of our profession, the women saints. They must be our patterns, as the Curé d'Ars is the pattern for the parish priest; so we ought to keep on looking at them, looking at the top, and note what they teach. They represent, each in their own intensely distinctive way, the classic norm of women's ministry. And the first thing we observe about them is that all are devoured by the immensity of their love and abandonment to God and Christ, and how all else flows from this and depends on their faithful, selfless, interior adherence. And next, I think, we notice a sort of beautiful informality and freedom in their proceedings, and something which we might call a maternal and domestic quality in their method, which seems on the whole to look more towards the prophetic than the priestly way of serving God and tending souls. We see them gathering little groups about them, creating spiritual families on whom they exercise a transforming power, giving people God in a very unofficial way. Of course we know and recognize that the Church needs both these types – they complete each other – but is it not here that women seem to find their best place? As individuals surrendered to the Spirit, moving and working under His pressure, and yet with great freedom and originality, within the institutional frame?

And next observe how quiet and hidden on the whole their best work is; and how sometimes when it develops and becomes public and they get a status – and especially when they begin to tell people in general what they ought to do and how things ought to be done, and the mother of souls becomes a reformer – they seem to charm us less, and tell us less of God. Most of us, I think, are definitely at our best in a limited environment; and it is only our best we want to give, isn't it? Our home-making talents and our instinct for nurture, teaching, loving – the power of concentrating on the individual, on the weak or the damaged, the intuitive touch on character and the understanding of it – these are the points at which women have something of real value to give to pastoral work. It is surely not when St Hildegarde becomes a public figure, a great woman, and enters the sphere of controversy, or when Elizabeth Fry makes a semi-royal progress through Europe, stiff with black silk and consciousness of her own vocation, that we feel them most to be agents of God. Then the interior simplicity on which all hangs seems to melt away. Even the great St Teresa said that her five happiest years were spent hidden away in the tiny convent of St Joseph, training her little group of daughters in the interior life.

Surely we want women to retain something of that precious suppleness, simplicity and freedom which makes us tools fit for many purposes. It is so much better just to be able to say 'Send me' without having to add 'where I shall have my position properly recognized, or opportunities to use my special gifts'. It is God whom we want to get recognized, not us. If we look again at the women saints, we see that with them that is usually so. They often had immense difficulties, emerging as most of them did within a Church far more rigidly organized than ours. They often suffered from the jealousy, misunderstanding and suspicion of their contemporaries. But they did feed some sheep; and that is what matters after all. Look at St Catherine in her little room at Siena, surrounded by her spiritual sons; or Madame Acarie fulfilling her vocation in and through her family life, and becoming the 'Conscience of Paris'. Consider those great lives, burning with charity; let us measure our thoughts about the ministry of women by them. A clear recognition of the standard they set is going to help women church workers through their ups and downs far better than any external change in our position can do. This change may turn out to be useful and desirable, but if the other side is lacking, it won't do much for the real life of the Church. All kinds of claimfulness are so foreign to the Christian genius that every movement of this kind involves a certain spiritual risk; whereas every movement towards humility and hiddenness actually increases our real value to God and the Church. This does not mean softness or inefficiency; it merely means leaving ourselves out.

Surely it is a good thing that the two orders of

service within the Church should be different; and there is a mass of social and spiritual work, teaching and guidance both individual and general, and detailed training in the interior life, in which it is certain that women can and should give far more service than they have yet done. The Church should welcome such ministry, and extend these opportunities. But even where the welcome is a little bit on the frosty side – for we know that the institutional mind is not always very elastic – that does not justify our making a fuss. In all those new developments of Christian method which must come, and ought to come, with changing times, I am sure that women should do, and will have to do, many new and responsible kinds of spiritual work in so far as they are fitted for it. But the fitness matters most; that interior poise which enables us to take any job, from the most desperate to the most homely, and link up the outward action with the unchanging Eternity whose purpose we are here to serve.

If a new era in women's life in the Church really is opening, do not let us come to it inwardly unprepared because we are in such a hurry to begin. I suppose, in the first century, the Church's need of workers was just as great as ours; but St Paul thought it was worthwhile to begin by hiding himself for three years in Arabia, in order that he might discover what the Spirit desired him to do. I have a feeling that we ought to do something like that. For improvement in our position, or the mere multiplication of women serving in the Church, will do nothing to extend the Kingdom unless those who enter on this career really are light-bringing souls, as von Hügel said; and they will only be that in proportion to their active self-abandonment, the extent in which they ignore their own preferences and so become sensitive to God.

So I think that efforts to defend and expand the ministry of women in the Church will be useless for the deeper purposes of the Spirit unless there is a ceaseless recognition that usefulness in religion means usefulness to God, and usefulness to God depends upon ceaseless co-operation with Him. And this again requires a sensitiveness to the movement of the Spirit impossible without a steady and disciplined interior life of prayer. I do not mean to suggest by this that the Spirit only acts through saints. The marvellous thing is that in the true ministry of Christendom God so constantly uses sinners; but I do think they have got to be very loving and grateful sinners, entirely free from any notions about the importance of their own status and their own work. If this temper of soul, this profound humility, is sought by us, then I should feel the future as regards the ministry of women was absolutely safe. Without it we should perhaps be wise to ponder the advice which the saintly Abbé Huvelin gave to a distinguished lady of our own communion who consulted him about her numerous religious activities: 'Madame, distrust your own zeal for doing good to others.'

THE HOUSE OF THE SOUL

⊙

WHEN ST PAUL DESCRIBED OUR MYSTERIOUS HUMAN nature as a 'temple of the Holy Spirit' – a created dwelling-place or sanctuary of the uncreated and invisible divine life – he was stating in the strongest possible terms a view of our status, our relation to God, which has always been present in Christianity and is indeed implicit in the Christian view of reality. But that statement as it stands seems far too strong for most of us. We do not feel in the very least like the temples of creative love. We are more at ease with St Teresa, when she describes the soul as an 'interior castle' – a roomy mansion, with various floors and apartments from the basement upwards, not all devoted to exalted uses, not always in a satisfactory state. And when, in a more homely mood, she speaks of her own spiritual life as 'becoming solid like a house', we at last get something we can grasp.

The soul's house, that interior dwelling-place which we all possess, for the upkeep of which we are responsible – a place in which we can meet God, or from which in a sense we can exclude God – that is not too big an idea for us. Though no imagery drawn from the life of sense can ever be adequate to the strange and delicate contacts, tensions, demands and benedictions of the life that lies beyond sense; though the important part of every parable is that which it fails to express; still, here is a conception which can be made to cover many of the truths that govern the interior life of prayer.

First, we are led to consider the position of the house. However interesting and important its peculiarities may seem to the tenant, it is not as a matter of fact an unusually picturesque and interesting mansion made to an original design and set in its own grounds with no other building in sight. Christian spirituality knows nothing of this sort of individualism. It insists that we do not inhabit detached residences but are parts of a vast spiritual organism, that even the most hidden life is never lived for itself alone. Our soul's house forms part of the vast City of God. Though it may not be an important mansion with a frontage on the main street, nevertheless it shares all the obligations and advantages belonging to the city as a whole. It gets its water from the main, and its light from the general supply. The way we maintain and use it must have reference to our civic responsibilities.

It is true that God creates souls in a marvellous liberty and variety. The ideals of the building estate tell us nothing about the Kingdom of Heaven. It is true, also, that the furnishing of our rooms and cultivation of our garden is largely left to our personal industry and good taste. Still, in a general way, we must fall in with the city's plan and consider, when we hang some new and startling curtains, how they will look from the street. However intense the personal life of each soul may be, that personal life has got out of proportion if it makes us forget our municipal obligations and advantages; for our true significance is more than personal, it is bound up with the fact of our status as members of a supernatural society. So into all the affairs of the little house there should enter a certain sense of the city, and beyond this of the infinite world in which the city stands: some awestruck memory of our double situation, at once so homely and so mysterious. We must each maintain unimpaired our unique relation with God; yet without forgetting our intimate contact with the rest of the city, or the mesh of invisible life which binds all the inhabitants in one.

For it is on the unchanging life of God, as on a rock, that the whole city is founded. That august and cherishing Spirit is the atmosphere which bathes it, and fills each room of every little house – quickening, feeding and sustaining. He is the one reality which makes us real; and, equally, the other houses too. 'If I am not in Thee', said St Augustine, 'then I am not at all.' We are often urged to think of the spiritual life as a personal adventure, a ceaseless hustle forward, with all its meaning condensed in the 'perfection' of the last stage. But though progress, or rather growth, is truly in it, such growth in so far as it is real can only arise from, and be conditioned by, a far more fundamental relation – the growing soul's abidingness in God.

Next, what type of house does the soul live in? It is a two-storey house. The psychologist too often assumes that it is a one-roomed cottage with a mud floor, and never even attempts to go upstairs. The extreme transcendentalist sometimes talks as though it were perched in the air, like the lake dwellings of our primitive ancestors, and had no ground floor at all. A more humble attention to facts suggests that neither of these simplifications is true. We know that we have a ground floor, a natural life biologically conditioned, with animal instincts and affinities, and that this life is very important, for it is the product of the divine creativity – its builder and maker is God. But we know too that we have an upper floor, a supernatural life with supernatural possibilities, a capacity for God, and that this, the peculiar prerogative of human beings, is more important still. If we try to live on one floor alone we destroy the mysterious beauty of our human vocation, so utterly a part of the fugitive and creaturely life of this planet and yet so deeply coloured by eternity, so entirely one with the world of nature and yet, 'in the Spirit', a habitation of God. 'Thou madest him lower than the angels, to crown him with glory and worship.' We are created both in time and in eternity, not truly one but truly two; and every thought, word and act must be subdued to the dignity of that double situation in which Almighty God has placed and companions the childish spirit of humanity.

Therefore a full and wholesome spiritual life can never consist in living upstairs and forgetting to consider the ground floor and its homely uses and needs, thus ignoring the humbling fact that those upper rooms are entirely supported by it. Nor does it consist in the constant, exasperated investigation of the shortcomings of the basement. When St Teresa said that her prayer had become 'solid like a house', she meant that its foundations now went down into the lowly but firm ground of human nature, the concrete actualities of the natural life, and on those solid foundations its wall rose up towards heaven. The strength of the house consisted in that intimate welding together of the divine and the human which she found in its perfection in the humanity of Christ. There, in the common stuff of human life which He blessed by His presence, the saints have ever seen the homely foundations of holiness. Since we are two-storey creatures, called to a natural and a supernatural status, both sense and spirit must be rightly maintained, kept in order, consecrated to the purposes of the city, if our full obligations are to be fulfilled. The house is built for God, to reflect, on each level, something of His unlimited Perfection. Downstairs, that general rightness of adjustment to all this-world obligations, which the ancients called the quality of justice, and the homely virtues of prudence, temperance and fortitude reminding us of our creatureliness, our limitations, and so humbling and disciplining us. Upstairs, the heavenly powers of faith, hope and charity, tending towards the eternal, nourishing our life towards God, and having no meaning apart from God.

But the soul's house will never be a real home unless the ground floor is as cared for and as habitable as the beautiful rooms upstairs. We are required to live in the whole of our premises, and are responsible for the condition of the whole of our premises. It is useless to repaper the drawing-room if what we really need is a new sink. In that secret divine purpose which is drawing all life towards perfection, the whole house is meant to be beautiful and ought to be beautiful, for it comes from God and was made to His design. Christ's soul when on earth lived in one of these houses, had to use the same fitments, make the same arrangements do. We cannot excuse our own failures by attributing them to the inconvenience of the premises, and the fact that some very old-fashioned bits of apparatus survive. Most of us have inherited some ugly bits of furniture, or unfortunate family portraits which we can't get rid of, and which prevent our rooms being quite a success. Nevertheless the soul does not grow strong merely by enjoying its upstairs privileges and ignoring downstairs disadvantages, problems and responsibilities, but only by tackling its real task of total transformation. It is called to maintain a house which shall be in its completeness 'a habitation of God in the Spirit', subdued to His purpose on all levels, manifesting His glory in what we call natural life as well as in what we call spiritual life. For humanity is the link between these two orders: truly created a little lower than the angels, yet truly crowned with glory and worship, because in this unperfected human nature the Absolute Life itself has deigned to dwell.

That means, reduced to practice, that the whole house with its manifold and graded activities must be a house of prayer. It does not mean keeping a Quiet Room to which we can retreat, with mystical pictures on the walls and curtains over the windows to temper the disconcerting intensity of the light, a room where we can forget the fact that there are black beetles in the kitchen, and that the range is not working very well. Once we admit any violent contrast between the upper and lower floor, the 'instinctive' and 'spiritual' life, or feel a reluctance to investigate the humbling realities of the basement, our life becomes less, not more, than human and our position is unsafe. Are we capable of the adventure of courage which inspires the great prayer of St Augustine: 'The house of my soul is narrow; do Thou enter in and enlarge it! It is ruinous; do Thou repair it'? Can we risk the visitation of the mysterious power that will go through all our untidy rooms, showing up their shortcomings and their possibilities, reproving by the tranquillity of order the waste and muddle of our inner life? The mere hoarded rubbish that ought to go into the dustbin; the things that want mending and washing; the possessions we have never taken the trouble to use? Yet this is the only condition on which human beings can participate in that fullness of life for which they are made.

The Lord's Prayer, in which St Teresa said that she found the whole art of contemplation from its simple beginning to its transcendent goal, witnesses with a wonderful beauty and completeness to this two-storey character of the soul's house, and yet its absolute unity. It begins at the top, in the watch-tower of faith, with the sublime assertion of our supernatural status – the one relation, intimate yet inconceivable, that governs all the rest – 'Our Father who art in Heaven, hallowed be *Thy* name.' Whatever the downstairs muddle and tension we have to deal with, however great the difficulty of adjusting the claims of the instincts that live in the basement and the interests that clamour at the door, all these demands, all this rich and testing experience is enfolded and transfused by the cherishing, overruling life and power of God. We are lifted clear of the psychological tangle in which the life of our spirit too often seems enmeshed, into the pure, serene light of eternity, and shown the whole various and disconcerting pageant of creation as proceeding from God and existing only that it may glorify His name. Childlike dependence and joyful adoration are placed together as the twin characters of the soul's relation to God.

Thence, step by step, this prayer brings us downstairs, goes with us through the whole house, bringing the supernatural into the natural, blessing and sanctifying, cleansing and rectifying every aspect of the home. 'Thy Kingdom come!' Hope – trustful expectation. 'Thy will be done!' Charity – the loving union of our wills with the Infinite Will. Then the ground floor. 'Give us this day' – that food from beyond ourselves which nourishes and sustains our life. Forgive all our little failures and excesses, neutralize the corroding power of our conflicts, disharmonies, rebellions, sins. We can't deal with them alone. Teach us, as towards our fellow citizens, to share that generous tolerance of God. Lead us not into situations where we are tried beyond our strength, but meet us on the battlefield of personality, and protect the weakness of the adolescent spirit against the downward pull of the inhabitants of the lower floor.

And then, the reason of all this, bringing together, in one supreme declaration of joy and confidence, the soul's sense of that supporting, holy, and eternal Reality who is the Ruler and the Light of the city, and of every room in every little house. Thine is the Kingdom, the power and the glory. If our interior life be subdued to the spirit of this prayer, with its rich sense of our mighty heritage and childlike status, our total dependence on the reality of God, then the soul's house is truly running well. Its action is transfused by contemplation. The door is open between the upper and the lower floors, the life of spirit and life of sense.

'Two cities', said St Augustine, 'have been created by two loves: the earthly city by love of self even to contempt of God, the heavenly city by love of God even to contempt of self. The one city glories in itself; the other city glories in the Lord. The one city glories in its own strength; the other city says to its God, "I will love Thee, O Lord my strength."' Perhaps there has never been a time in Christian history when that contrast has been more sharply felt than it is now – the contrast between that view of the human situation and meaning in which the emphasis falls on humanity, its vast desires and wonderful achievements, even to contempt of God; and the view in which the emphasis falls on God's transcendent action and overruling will, even to contempt of self. St Augustine saw, and still would see, humanity ever at work building those two cities, and every human soul as a potential citizen of one or the other. And from this point of view, that which we call the 'interior life' is just the home life of those who inhabit the invisible City of God, realistically taking up their municipal privileges and duties and pursuing them 'even to contempt of self'. It is the obligation and the art of keeping the premises entrusted to us in good order, having ever in view the welfare of the city as a whole.

Some souls, like some people, can be slummy anywhere. There is always a raucous and uncontrolled voice ascending from the basement, and a pail of dirty water at the foot of the stairs. Others can achieve in the most impossible situation a simple and beautiful life. The good citizen must be able without reluctance to open the door at all times, not only at the weekend; must keep the windows clean and taps running properly, that the light and living water may come in. These free gifts of the supernatural are offered to each house, and only as free gifts can they be had. Our noisy little engine will not produce the true light, nor our most desperate digging a proper water supply. Recognition of this fact, this entire dependence of the creature, is essential if the full benefits of our mysterious citizenship are ever to be enjoyed by us. 'I saw', said the poet of the Apocalypse, 'the holy city coming *down* from God out of heaven . . . the glory of God lit it . . . the water of life proceeded out of the throne of God.' All is the free gift of the super-natural, not the result of human growth and effort. God's generous and life-giving work in the world of souls ever goes before humanity's work in God. So the main thing about the Invisible City is not the industry and good character of the inhabitants; they do not make it shine. It is the tranquil operation of that perpetual providence which incites and supports their small activities; the direct and childlike relation in which they stand to the city's Ruler; the generous light and air that bathe the little houses; the unchanging rock of eternity on which their foundations stand.

INDEX